g

Random Thoughts about Life, Love

Revell
Grand Rapids, Michigan

& Relationships

Justin Lookadoo

© 2007 by Justin Lookadoo

Published by Fleming H. Revell
a division of Baker Publishing Group
P.O. Box 6287, Grand Rapids, MI 49516-6287
www.revellbooks.com

Printed in the United States of America

Library of Congress Cataloging-in-Publication Data
Lookadoo, Justin.
    97 : random thoughts about life, love, and relationships /
Justin Lookadoo.
        p.   cm.
    ISBN 10: 0-8007-3163-8 (pbk.)
    ISBN 978-0-8007-3163-2 (pbk.)
    1. Preteens—Religious life—Juvenile literature. 2. Preteens—
Prayer-books and devotions—English—Juvenile literature. 3.
Christian life—Juvenile literature. I. Title
BV4870.L66 2007
248.8′3—dc22   2006036542

interior design by Brian Brunsting

CON

TENTS

Introd

Here you have it. The book you've been waiting for and didn't even know it. Wipe your tears away and stop hounding the lady at the bookstore, because you've got the book in your mitts.

97 is a journey—a mystical look into the deep recesses of your soul—that will infiltrate your core and ignite your hidden passions. Okay, not really. But it would be cool if it were.

Actually, it's exactly what the subtitle says it is: random thoughts about life, love, and relationships. And it's not just any random thoughts. These are the best of the best. Nothing is sacred and nothing really has to make sense. Why? Because it's my book and it's a peek inside my head, and in there, nothing is sacred and not a lot of things make sense.

As I have studied what makes a book good, I have discovered a common thread. It is that no good book is complete without an appearance by a hot chica. One that acts distant but secretly desires the hero (that's me). A woman to make me believe that I'm the playa I tell myself I am. So I got the girl who put the "pur" in *purdee*—my wife and soon to be your friend, Emily Lookadoo.

Applause

If you've heard me speak, then you'll know Emily as my "loud-mouthed, skydiving, weight-lifting wife." If cool was a hot-air balloon, she would be the Goodyear blimp. She's that cool. And more than that, she is filled with twisted visions and thoughts that allow her to see God in some pretty amazing ways. She will hit you with some here in 97.

uction

Also making her first appearance in Lookadoo bux is a longtime friend of mine. She is 24 years old and a Capricorn. She enjoys cake decorating and long walks on the beach. Give a warm welcome to Brooke Wilson.

And finally, a man who needs no introduction . . . so I won't. Thank you for buying this book and I hope . . . oh, alright, I'll introduce him. A gazillion-album-selling singer/songwriter who has enough awards to cover the Great Wall of China. A family man, youth pastor, and fellow ADD author. Give it up for the writings of Casting Crowns front man Mr. Mark Haaaaaalllllllll.

And there you have it. The starring cast of 97. The next few pages are the masterpieces of wit, wisdom, and wishes from the dream team. It will be the book you will want to come back to all year long. So get ready to enjoy, mark up, tear out, and own the thoughts we bring to you in this steaming pile of wonderful.

Once you're done absorbing the words, get out there and share your freshly learned awesomeness with the world. It would be selfish to keep it all to yourself.

Cheer

Wild Whoop

See you on the flip side . . .
of the paper.
Get it? Just turn the page.

Some people called him George, some called him Mr. Gross, but the only thing I ever called him is *Pa*. He was my grandfather, and I was his oldest grandson.

Pa was a farmer during a time when farmers didn't make much money. (Yeah, like they're rollin' in it now.) He was a hardworking man. Not much of a formal education but very wise. I learned to drive sitting in his lap. In fact, I can't remember an age when I wasn't behind the wheel of his pickup. I was out of his lap and on my own by age 9. His farm is where I learned how to hoe weeds, brand cattle, pull fence, grow peppers, and most of all to see the world in a new and exciting way.

> I also learned valuable lessons like, *Don't pee on an electric fence. Skunks don't make good pets. Just because the hogs play in it doesn't mean you should.* All very important things for a young boy to learn.

I remember the summer I didn't go see my grandfather. I was in college; I had my life going. I was focused on my future and having a blast in the moment. I thought about going to see him, but the plane ticket would cost me $97. Yeah, not a biggie, right? Well, if you are a broke, busy, me-centered college student, it's a hugantic amount of money. I decided that I would have to wait. I would save up the cash and go see him at Thanksgiving.

Several weeks after I ditched my granddad because of lack of dough, I got the phone call. Mom said that Pa was dead. He worked all day just like he always did, he came home and lay down on the couch to take a nap, and he never woke up.

I broke down. I didn't get to say good-bye. I needed one more glimpse. One more lesson. One more ride on the tractor. One more conversation with my Pa. But it would never happen. And I missed it because of $97. That was what kept me from seeing my grandfather before he died: $97. It seemed like way too much money then, but now it's nothing. I couldn't believe that I lost my last chance to see Pa because of a measly $97.

Every time I think about that, I get sick. I can't believe I let something stand in my way. I can't believe I blew it so easily. But I don't let it beat me down. That sick feeling I get is a huge reminder. It drives me and motivates me to never let anything get in the way of doing what I know is right. It fuels me to keep going when things are tough. It supercharges me when I see something trying to slow me down.

In fact, 97 is my number. I keep it everywhere. That way when I think I need to call someone, talk with someone, send them an email, and I want to be lazy and blow it off till later . . . 97. When I see something happening that I know is wrong, and I can do something about it, but it would be so much easier to sit back and not get involved . . . 97. When I don't want to even get out of bed because I am bummed out about life . . . 97.

Step up. Make a difference. Reach out. Go see your grandparents. Give a dollar to the dude. Don't let anything get in your way of doing what needs to be done. 97!

This book is all about you stepping up.

It's all about you digging deeper, growing bigger, and living with no regrets.

This book is your road to 97.

US
97

Grabbin' a Snak

"To a fool, a little knowledge is a dangerous thing." Yep, and I am proof that this saying is true.

I love the animal shows on TV. I was watching one of the funny-talking dudes and he was doing an entire special on poisonous snakes. He would run after them and grab 'em by the tail and lift them off the ground with his arm sticking way out. I thought it was a stupid move, but hey, he's the pro, plus he said only two snakes in the world can double up above them-

Well, there I was sitting in my chair, looking out the back door, when all of a sudden a six-foot snake went slithering across my porch, heading straight to the back room of the house. I knew exactly what to do. I shot out of my chair and ran outside. I reached down and grabbed the snake by the tail just like TV man did. I stuck my arm out with confidence and heard his voice in my head, "Only two snakes in the world can double up over themselves and strike. One is the black mamba and the

the snake and started spinning around and around. I figured no snake in the world can double up when it is riding the tilt-o-whirl. I positioned myself in a perfect line with my door. I got my rhythm going, and at the right moment, I let the snake go sailing across the yard. And like a fearless he-man, I turned and ran toward the door, went in the house, and locked the door like he would come walking up trying to pick the lock.

I never said I was smart. Like the ancient Proverb says,

selves to bite you, so he was safe.

I was soaking up all this info not just because it was cool but also because I had been having problems with snakes getting into my house. Not cute, cuddly snakes. I am talking poisonous water moccasin monsters. In fact, one snuck into the back room and decided to shed his skin. When I spread the skin across the floor it was eight feet long. Eight freaking feet long and it was in my house! *Auuuuugggggghhhh-hhhh!*

other is . . ." and my mind went blank. "And the other is . . ." I can't remember! What was the second snake? Was it the water moccasin? Here I am holding the tail of a poisonous snake and I cannot remember if this was the other one that could double up on itself.

What now? Don't panic. I will just put him back on the ground. No, he's six feet long and pretty ticked off, and he could come after me. Okay, I could hold it and . . . no, it may be snake number two. Okay, panic! I took

"The way of a fool seems right to him, but a wise man listens to advice." Yeah, there I was, the poster boy of chapter 12, verse 15. But all of this did teach me a little something. It taught me to get the full story. Before I start making plans, passing judgment, or talking about someone, I need to make sure I get the full scoop. Don't just jump on the judgmental express to slanderville. Otherwise, this may be the one that doubles back and bites.

Hot or Not

Which Are You?

**Hey there, ya hottie. You are F.I.N.E.
Just let me look at you. Beautiful!**

If you are like most of us, when you read that you turn around, looking to see who I'm talking to. Can't be you. You probably believe that you are "too." *Too* fat. *Too* tall. *Too* short, *too* skinny, *too* white, *too* dark . . . *too*. And you know what? You're right.

Okay, not the most compassionate thing to say, but oh well. Here's the deal. The only reason you are *too* anything is because of what you are comparing yourself *to*. And you will always see yourself as being too something if you continue to compare.

I'm 6 foot 7. And most of my life I feel like I am too tall. Yeah, the short people out there are saying, "There's no such thing as too tall." Okay, except when you try to fly in a plane, or buy clothes that fit, or ride the rides at an amusement park, or walk through a room with ceiling fans. So yeah, for the most part I feel too tall.

Until . . . I go hang out with a pro basketball team. Then the whole world changes. No longer am I the tall goofy guy who is self-conscious about his height, but I am the short goofy guy, feeling weird about being the "short guy."

Listen, the way you feel about your body has very little to do with your bod. It has a lot to do with what you are comparing yourself to. Check it: If you want to change the way you feel, then stop looking around to see how you rate and start looking up to your Creator. He made you the way you are. Look at you through the loving eyes of the Father, and it will change the way you feel about you.

Warning: While looking to find your acceptance from God, don't fall into the Excuse Zone. For example, if you don't like yourself because you are overweight, and meanwhile you sit at home watching TV, slamming down tubs of B&J ice cream, only getting enough exercise to get you back to the refrig . . . c'mon. This has nothing to do with comparison. It has everything to do with ignoring the fact that your body is the temple of God. So don't blame that on "this is just the way God made me." Get a grip and take control of your life.

But on the flip side, maybe you are one of those people who are just skinny. No matter how much you eat or work out, you never seem to get past the "boney" stage, then come to God and ask him to give you his eyes. In fact, that is the deal with just about every body image issue. Start by going to God and telling him what you feel you are "too." Ask him if it is true and what you should do. Then wait for an answer. God made you, and he wants you to see yourself with all the love and acceptance *he* sees you with. When you get down on yourself, hold on to Psalm 139:14: "I praise you because I am fearfully and wonderfully made." That's you. Fearfully and wonderfully made by the Creator of that which is perfectly made . . . you.

Do you wish you could get your parents to loosen up a little? To ease up and give you a little more freedom? Well, it can happen. But your only chance for success requires completely understanding the anatomy of the parental brain.

First you must understand why parents act the way they do. And Proverbs 22:6 gives us a glimpse of their reasoning when it says, "Train a child in the way he should go, and when he is old he will not turn from it." Parents have a two-part agenda:

1. Train the child

2. Make sure he/she lives to be old

These two overlapping goals control how parents act.

Next you must dig deep into the anatomy of the parental brain to understand how it functions.

The parental brain is made up of four primary regions: Nosey Lobe (NL), Worry Region (WR), Safety Cortex (SC), and Myduty Ijustgottaknowa (MI). Each one functions individually yet also is a part of the capacity of the brain as a whole. Notice the differences and how each one affects the others.

Here is a brief description of how the parental brain functions (see illustration 94a): The information they receive through the Nosey Lobe and the Myduty Ijustgottaknowa are processed through the Worry Region and then translated by the Safety Cortex. The results are seen in the form of rules and regulations such as curfews, dress restrictions, and pal preferences.

Dilemma

As you get older you need more freedom to grow, develop, and become your

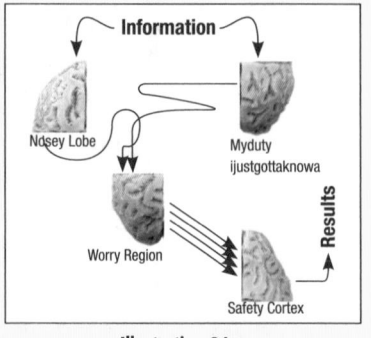

Illustration 94a

own person. But during these teen years the Worry Region and Safety Cortex become extremely active due to the current stupidity of teens in general or parents' remembrance of their own lack of good judgment during those years.

Solution

You must rewire your parent's brain. The key to gaining more freedom and more trust is feeding your parents more information. By increasing the amount of info you input in the Nosey Lobe and the Myduty Ijustgottaknowa, you will help stabilize the activity of the Safety Cortex and the Worry Region.

Here's How It Works

Normal Teen Situation: You are going out Friday night and you and your parents go through your normal routine. They begin . . .

PARENT: "Where are you going?"
YOU: "Out."
PARENT: "Out where?"
YOU: "Movies."
PARENT: "What movie?"
YOU: "Scooby Doo 4."

Nosey Lobe (NL)

This area of the brain is the same in all parents. They are naturally nosey. This area controls the appetite for seemingly useless and meaningless information. It is activated by the mere fact that they are a parent. Some parents have overactive nosey lobes, which produces excessive question-asking and prying into your business. But overall this area is quite mellow.

Worry Region (WR)

This region is more highly developed in the female parent. The male species has equal worry functioning; however, it is released as a long, slow twitch, while the female releases a fast twitch. This means a female will respond with worry much quicker than a male and will sustain low-grade worry throughout her life. For a male, worry takes longer to build, but once the threshold has been reached, his worry will be more intense and more difficult to subdue.

Safety Cortex (SC)

This section of the parental brain was activated when you were born and will lessen somewhat over the years but never cease to function. A mother is activated by a need to care for and nurture her child. A father's safety cortex is one part care and nurture, three parts wanting to know whose body he will need to hide if something happens to you. In both parents the activity of this region is increased when you face any real or perceived danger.

Myduty Ijustgottaknowa (MI)

This is the central functioning system of a parent's brain. The need to know comes from the simple fact that *I am the parent and I have a right to know. I provide the roof over your head, the food you eat, the clothes you wear, and the money you spend, so that makes me in charge.*

PARENT: "Where?"
YOU: "Theater."
PARENT: "What theater?"
YOU: "MoviePlex 5."
PARENT: "What time is it over?"
YOU: "9:30."
PARENT: "Who are you going with?"
YOU: "Friends."
PARENT: "What friends?"
YOU: "Erin, Nikki, Blake."
PARENT: "Who's taking you and picking you up?"
YOU: "Blake's mom."

Notice that with each question that is asked, the Nosey Lobe tells the Myduty Ijustgottaknowa that you must be hiding something. The Myduty Ijustgottaknowa sends a signal to the Worry Region, which begins to increase the worry, initiating a tighter enforcement of the rules by the Safety Cortex.

If you want to reverse this cycle, you do it with information. And here's how. Take the same teen situation: You are going out Friday night. But this time you implement your new strategy of parental brain rewiring.

PARENT: "Where are you going?"

YOU: "Hey, I'm going to the movies tonight with Erin, Nikki, and Blake. We're going to the MoviePlex 5 to see *Scooby Doo 4*. It starts at 7:45 and ends around 9:30. Blake's mom is taking us and picking us up. We're going to stop for ice cream on the way home, so we should be home by 10:15."

All parent brain function will cease for a brief moment. Give them some time to recover and process everything you just said. It may seem strange to them because the Nosey Lobe and Myduty Ijustgottaknowa have been satisfied, so the Worry Region and Safety Cortex are not cued into motion.

At first you may find your parents asking questions you have already answered or questions that don't really relate to anything. This is because you have short-circuited their normal brain function. It may take them some time to stop this. Repeat the process enough times to give them imprinted memories to draw from, and then you will have created a foundation that allows you to ask for more freedoms and responsibilities.

Reaction Warning: Upon receiving your new freedom, be sure to conform to the new boundaries without exception. If your curfew is increased to 11:45, *make sure* you get home before then. Not doing so will cause adverse reactions that could result in overstimulation of the Safety Cortex and Worry Region, thereby reversing all previous advancements and increasing the difficulty of gaining any future freedoms.

This process may take some time to master. But if you are persistent, the rewards will be far greater than any effort you put in. You will grow more and more as an adult, and your parents will be more confident that you:

1. Have been trained
2. Will live to get old

The Broken Road

observations from Emily Lookadoo

There's nothing a girl can do—and no guy she can find—that will give her that perfect feeling inside. Only God can do that. So trying to get it yourself—or find a someone to give it to you—is time ill spent on the road. You know, God has given you this time in your life for a reason. Some girls sit back and they wait and they wait and they wait for Prince Charming. That's not supposed to be an idle time. God doesn't expect you to sit there and pray that Prince Charming will fall into your lap. Nor does he expect you to give everybody a shot at that role. He doesn't at all want you to sit idly waiting. He wants you to use this time to get to know him and to experience life with him.

Used to be I didn't understand that. And that left a gap in my life that I regret. Because while Justin was learning other languages and developing his relationship with God and writing books and doing meaningful things, I was trying one more hairdo, one more color, one more outfit. And I was constantly not hitting my mark.

You will be pretty enough, you will be perfect enough only when you see yourself through God's eyes. And then when you find your knight in shining armor at the end of the road, you will be perfect enough. You will be beautiful. There's no way that Justin would have ever found me without God's hand in my life. I'm glad I finally figured that out.

Santa's Tips for Back to School

Summer is all but done and school is on its way—not nearly as much fun as Santa, but just as inevitable. But as the bikinis and boards are being put away, there is good news: A new school year can mean a new you. You get to go back to school a different person. And to do this, let's get a few tricks from dear ol' Santa.

1. Make a list and check it twice. Write down all the things you want to accomplish this school year: "Make A's and B's in all my classes. Be in the school play. Start a Bible study. Get along with all my teachers." Then make a plan for how you are going to make it happen. Check it: An ancient proverb says, "In his heart a man plans his course, but the LORD determines his steps." You gotta have a plan.

1 Corinthians 15:33

2. See who's naughty or nice. You wanna know who you are, then look at the people you hang with. If you see them as partiers, liars, and backstabbers, then that is how everyone sees you. If the friendventory shows they are people with solid character, compassion for others, and a passion for life, that's probably who you are too. You may think your pals don't affect who you are, but listen, "Bad company corrupts good character." So if your buds are making you a better person, they're keepers. If they are tearing you down, let 'em go. It's better to find new friends than to keep ones that will hurt you.

Luke 6:38

3. Give gifts and toys to girls and boys. The best way to feel good about you is to focus on someone else. If you have ever gone on a mission trip or done a humanitarian project, you catch this vibe. You go there with the attitude that you are really gonna help some folks, and you come back with your life changed. This works on a daily level here at home too. If there is a kid at school that nobody likes, eat lunch with him. Sneak the grouchy history teacher a note that says, "You are my fave. Thanks for teaching me." Don't sign it. Just let him bask in knowing that someone thinks he is doing a great job. You will be amazed at what happens when you and your buds start trying to out-give each other. And there is a major bonus to giving, as Jesus pointed out way back in the first century: "Give, and it will be given to you. A good measure, pressed down, shaken together and running over, will be poured into your lap. For with the measure you use, it will be measured to you."

Yeah, it's way too early to be thinking about Santa, but using some of his ideas will make your school year a blowout success. Good luck and Vaya con Dios.

Ice Walker

START

Jesus is the hottest thing going right now. He has hit pop icon superstardom. From books, movies, and T-shirts to TV shows and scientific explorations. He has even shown up in a few rap videos.

Don't get all holy roller on us now. He is not there because of his miracles, his message, or his messiah-ness. He hit the stratosphere because of his marketability. Yeah, you've heard people say "sex sells." Well, go ahead and guerrilla glue that tagline onto the Son of God . . . *Jesus sells.*

We could waste our air debating if that is right or wrong, but really, I don't care. It has been interesting, though, to watch everyone jumping on the Jesus bandwagon. In fact, many people are riding this wave of popularity while trying to prove that the wave is wrong.

Look it. A professor of oceanography from Florida named Doron Nof says that he has studied the weather patterns, and his theory is that Jesus didn't walk on water. He says that it was cold and winter and Jesus actually was walking on ice. Wow, that sounds logical and so easy . . . until you actually read the whole story. What Mr. Ice Theory Man did was just pull out one piece of the picture and focus on it without any relation to anything else.

Read the story. This won't take long, and you'll see how easy it is to disprove the skeptics if you just know a little bit of the Bible.

Grab a Bible and read Matthew 14:22–33. C'mon, the rest of this won't make any sense if you don't know the story. It's a quick read. Go.

If that was the way it happened, don't you think it would have been newsworthy enough to make somebody's list? Don't you think one of the guys journaling about their life with Jesus would have written, *Dear Diary, today was insane. You know how crazy Peter is. Well, Jesus came walking out to our boat, and Peter thought he was walking on water. So Pete jumped out and tried to do the same. There were ice chunks all around the boat, so Peter jumped off the boat onto one of the chunks. Idiot. Of course the chunk just shot out from under him. He went straight into the freezing water. The waves were too harsh for him to get back in the boat. Jesus had to move from chunk to chunk until he got close enough to pull Peter out from the water. The water was super cold, duh, and Peter did not pass go, he went straight to hypothermia. We finally got him in the boat, and luckily we had Jesus there, because he did that whole healing thing that he does and got Pete warmed up. . . . Man, what a day.*

But alas, nothing. The moral of the story: Don't believe everything you hear. Take it back to the Word and then ask a few simple questions. For the most part you won't have to defend the Bible from people. Just ask some quick questions about their theory and they will sink as fast as Peter did when he started to freak out about the waves and stopped looking at Jesus.

This is all about becoming strong in your faith. Don't let spiritual bullies push you around. Get strong and get in the Word.

END

Have you ever tried to balance on a float or life jacket or anything that's in the water? Now imagine there's a huge storm, waves are blowing like crazy, you are having to grab another person, and both of you have to jump from floaty to floaty until you get to a boat.

So the boat was not on a sheet of ice. I can accept that. Then how did Peter jump off the boat and walk on water? Did he balance on the ice chunks, and is that why he began to sink? And then what about when Jesus reached down and got him out of the water—did they both balance on ice chunks and hopscotch back to the boat?

Just reading the story and thinking about Nof's theory, did you see anything that made you think, *Hmm, that doesn't make sense?* Think about it. Where are the major holes?

Here are a few of my little brainy Qs: If the water was frozen, then how could the boat be cruising through the water? Did they put skis on the bottom and let the wind blow it across? Okay, probably not. But a possible explanation to that is that boats are much heavier than people, so a boat would be able to break through where a person would not.

Spring has sprung and love is in the air. Doesn't it feel good to get outta the layers of clothes that have been hiding you from the hotties and go find your made-to-order soul mate? But be careful. You have to take some precautions before you jump into the relational deep end.

1. *Wait 30 minutes after eating.* Yeah, you gotta let the grub settle before you swim with the dolphins. The same with your crush. Don't jump into a super-exclusive relationship immediately after meeting this person. I mean, look what happened to Samson. He got his head shaved and lost all his strength. Take the time to let things settle. Get control of your emotions, step back, and look at the facts. Many times that person we meet on the beach by the campfire in the dark when the mood is just right seems to be our missing piece. But then when we wait a little while, we notice they are not our missing piece, they are just missing a few pieces.

Read all about it in Judges 16

DATEABLE

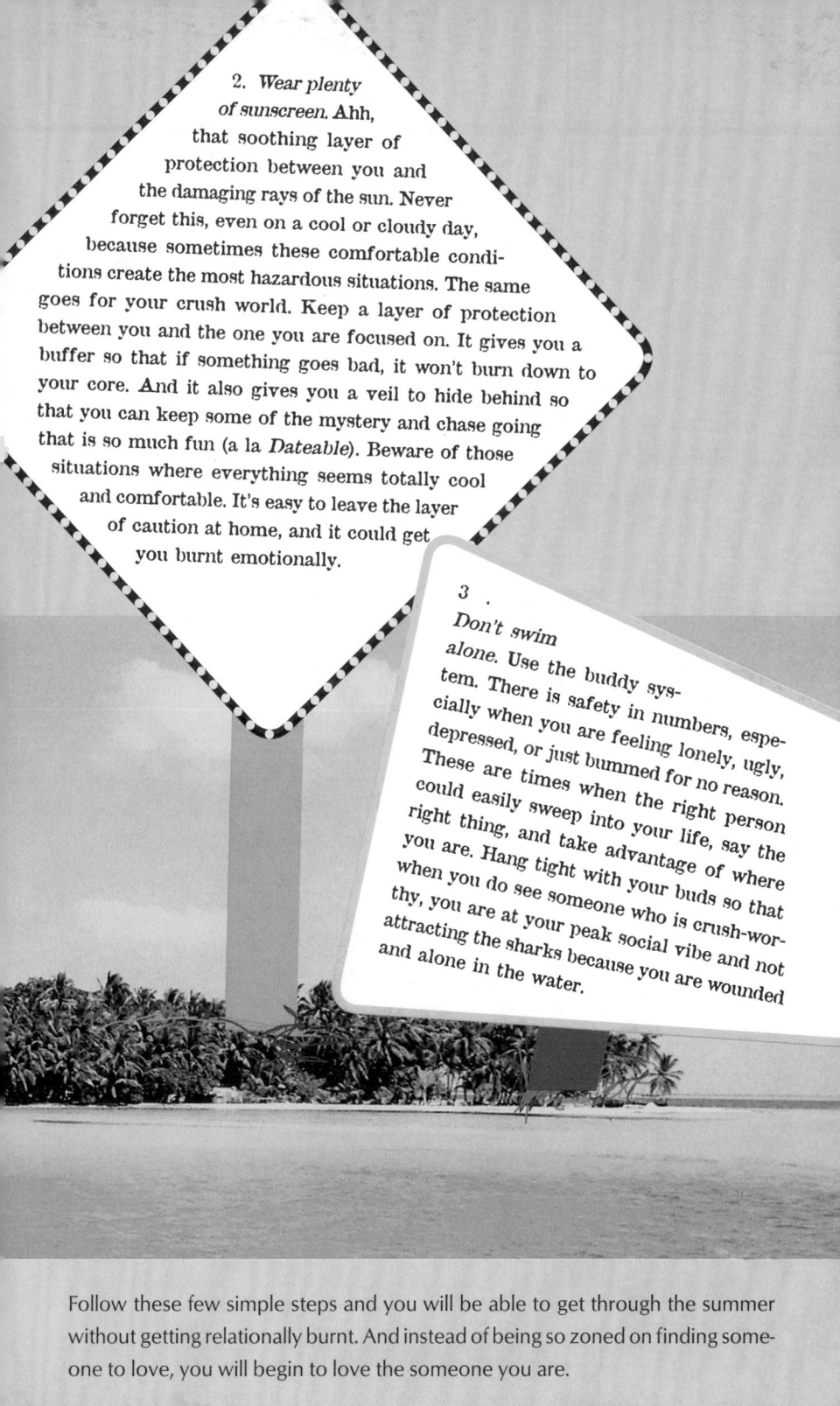

2. *Wear plenty of sunscreen.* Ahh, that soothing layer of protection between you and the damaging rays of the sun. Never forget this, even on a cool or cloudy day, because sometimes these comfortable conditions create the most hazardous situations. The same goes for your crush world. Keep a layer of protection between you and the one you are focused on. It gives you a buffer so that if something goes bad, it won't burn down to your core. And it also gives you a veil to hide behind so that you can keep some of the mystery and chase going that is so much fun (a la *Dateable*). Beware of those situations where everything seems totally cool and comfortable. It's easy to leave the layer of caution at home, and it could get you burnt emotionally.

3. *Don't swim alone.* Use the buddy system. There is safety in numbers, especially when you are feeling lonely, ugly, depressed, or just bummed for no reason. These are times when the right person could easily sweep into your life, say the right thing, and take advantage of where you are. Hang tight with your buds so that when you do see someone who is crush-worthy, you are at your peak social vibe and not attracting the sharks because you are wounded and alone in the water.

Follow these few simple steps and you will be able to get through the summer without getting relationally burnt. And instead of being so zoned on finding someone to love, you will begin to love the someone you are.

It's a Character

Character. That is one of the most beat down, misunderstood words out there. If you've been anywhere near a school in the last ten years, you've heard "character" thrown around like a baseball in Little League. We even have "Character Ed" classes. Class to teach character? You gotta be kidding me.

Skip the class. Scrap the textbook. I will save you a semester of your life and give you the most basic, simple definition of character: *Character is doing the right thing just because it's the right thing.* Not because it's cool, it's popular, or it's good. It's just doing it because it's right.

If you have never thought about your character or your friends' character, I'll tell you how to figure it out right now. Character is the choice you would make if you knew you would never get caught. What would you do if you knew you'd never get busted for it? That is your character.

Break it down a little further. If I will do it for you, I will do it to you. Let that ooze through your brain for a second. If I will do it *for* you, I will do it *to* you. It's a character issue.

Listen, if you have a group of friends and whenever someone in the group is not there right at that moment, everyone else is

Thing

"Let your 'Yes' be yes and your 'No,' no."

James 5:12

talking trash about them . . . guess what they're doing to you when you're not around? Yep, exact same thing. It's a character issue.

If one of your friends will lie to keep you guys out of trouble, you can't believe a word they say. They are a liar. It's a character thing. Whenever they are uncomfortable with telling the truth, they will lie. And that means to you too.

Check your friends. Check your character. If you don't like what you see then it's time to change. And remember to do the right thing just because it's right.

88

Duck ~~Glory~~ → Glory

There I was sitting on the banks of a river in South Texas, trying to write a book and arguing with God. I asked him what he wanted me to do. His God-response was, "Bring glory to me." Yeah, great church answer, God. What does that mean?

He said, "Do what I made you to do. That is how you bring glory to me."

I said, "You made me a speaker, not a writer. I was made to speak, so if I am going to bring glory to you, I need to quit this writing crap and get to speaking."

"Right now, you're a writer. So right now, if you are going to bring me glory, you'd better start writing. Everything in existence brings me glory by being what it is made to be. See that duck?" I looked out and there was a duck on a rock in the middle of the river. God said, "That duck is bringing me glory. It's not trying to be a fish or a tree. It's just being a duck. It is doing what I made it to do, so I am getting the glory."

Kinda like what it says in 1 Corinthians 7:20. Each one should remain in the situation which he was in when God called him.

Right at that moment the duck shot a line of poop out halfway across the rock. I fell over laughing. I said, "Hey God, did that give you some glory?"

"Yep," he said, "because that's what ducks do. Now shut up and start writing."

What has God made you to do? What has he put in front of you or given you the talents or opportunities for? If you want to truly glorify the one who made you, then go do it. And if whatever it is changes, then go do that. Don't try to be something you're not. Be only what God has made you to be. And remember the duck—he was a holy duck and was totally living by the Word of God: "So whether you eat or drink or poop or whatever you do, do it all for the glory of God."

1 Corinthians 10:31

CHURCH:
VIDEO GAME FOR THE SOUL

Skydiving is taking a hit . . . oops, bad wordage. But it is. In fact, almost all extreme sports are losing traction. Fewer people are getting into them. Why? Oh, I'm so glad the little voice in my head asked. One of the major thoughts is because of video games.

Extreme sports happen outside. They require something from you. It seems that more and more people are playing video games *about* doing something instead of actually *doing* it. In fact, that's what all video games are. They are *about* doing something and not *doing* it. And you know, these gamers may be onto something.

If you get up and do something, especially an extreme sport, it requires something of you. It requires that you dig deep into yourself and take risks.

You risk being made fun of. You risk rejection, and hey, a big risk—pain. You risk losing without the safety net of a reset button.

You know, I think for a lot of people the church has become a religious video game. We go, we sit, we experience. It's where we hear *about* changing the world. It's where we hear *about* our power. It's where we hear *about* God's plan for our life, *about* living our life with full-on abandonment . . . but we don't *do* it, because doing it would take a huge risk. Risk of losing control. Risk of having to change, of being made fun of. Yeah, we would rather talk *about* living for God than actually risk everything and *do* it.

Don't you think it's time to drop the controller, get off the couch, and play a real game? Just a thought . . .

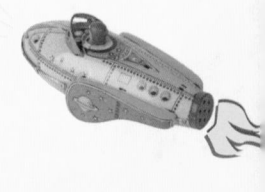

"Then Jesus said to his disciples, 'If anyone would come after me, he must deny himself and take up his cross and follow me. For whoever wants to save his life will lose it, but whoever loses his life for me will find it. What good will it be for a man if he gains the whole world, yet forfeits his soul? Or what can a man give in exchange for his soul?'"

Matthew 16:24–26

#86 REDNECK GOD

There is proof that God is a redneck. Honest-to-goodness proof. And it is the duck-billed platypus. I mean, look at it. It's made out of duct tape, bailing wire, and leftover parts.

I would have loved to be in the planning meeting. I can just hear God shouting (best read out loud in your most obnoxious redneck voice):

"Hey, boys, I think we have enough stuff to build one more thing. Bring me that duck bill. What else do we have? A beaver tail? Yeah, bring that too. What about that mammal fur, we got enough? Bring those leftover webbed feet while you're at it. Ah, yeah. That's looking good. Oh, for fun, just to mess with people's heads, let's make it lay eggs like a chicken. Yeah, that's it. And just to teach people that they shouldn't laugh at my creations, let's hide some little poisonous claws on him. Not enough to kill a human, but enough to let you know he got you. Perfect. Send him down to Earth."

Okay, I don't know if the db platy is enough to prove God is a redneck, but it sure does prove that he's creative. He can come up with some seriously messed-up stuff.

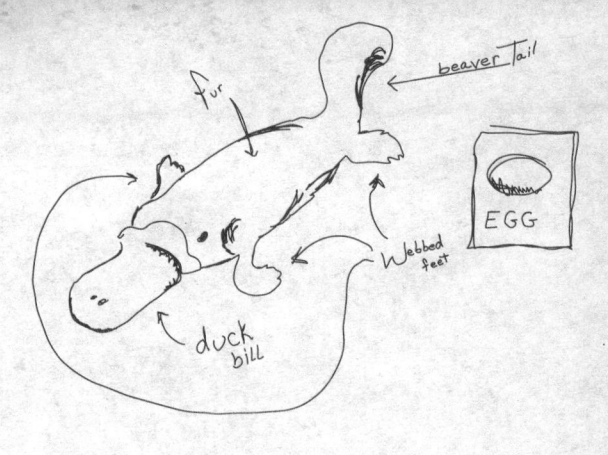

You know what? If you are in a sitch where you really think God wants you to do something but it just doesn't make sense, go do it anyway. He may have something going that is way cool and way out of our mentalsphere to comprehend. In fact, it's pretty much a sure thing. Check out 1 Corinthians 2:9: *No eye has seen, no ear has heard, no mind has conceived what God has prepared for those who love him.*

The Bible is full of that stuff. Stuff that doesn't make sense. Like, the enemy is coming to kill God's people, so "Moses, go stand by the water and hold up your stick." Huh? There's a mob of hungry people to feed, so "Hey, bring me that boy's sack lunch. Yeah, a couple of fish sticks and some biscuits—now go feed those 5,000 people with it." Huh? You'll never get to the WOW! if you don't power through the HUH? Hey, I like that. I'm gonna say it again.

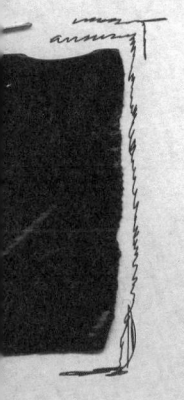

You'll never get to the WOW! if you don't power through the HUH?

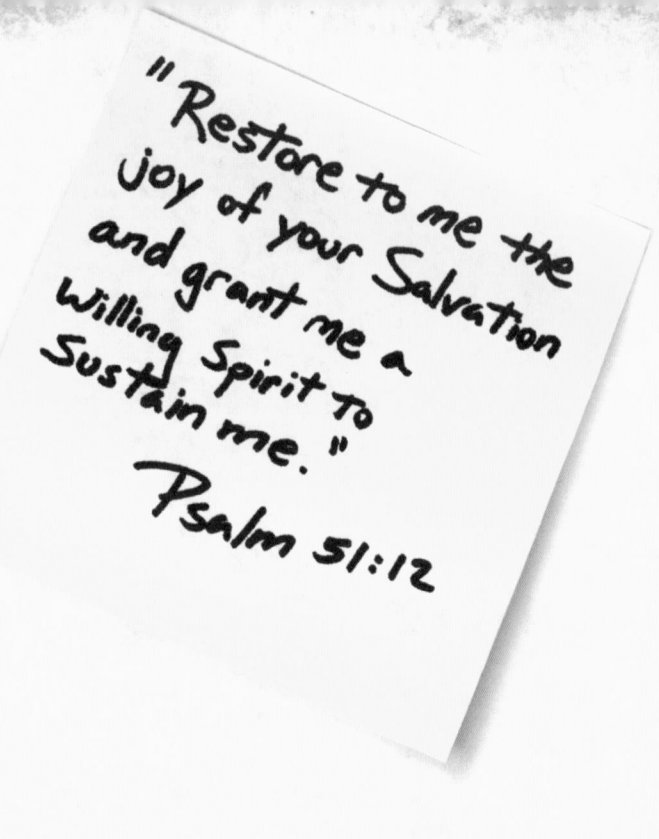

"Restore to me the Joy of your Salvation and grant me a willing Spirit To Sustain me."

Psalm 51:12

#85 Do-Over!

Today is the day you start over.

It's the first day of the new you.

So, what would you like to redo? Want to reinvent yourself and become a different person? Today is your day. Did you make some kind of commitment to someone, to yourself, to God that you've been slackin' on? Do-over! Have you been a Mean Girl? Been slipping back into porn? Blew your exercise program? Shruggin' off spending time with God?

Whatever your deal is, today is the day to declare a do-over and start again. Right now make one decision that will get you rolling toward the new you. It doesn't matter how big or small it is. Just do something to get the momentum going. Get a plan and start again. Today is Day 1.

DO-OVER! Prayer

Pray a little something like this.

God, I want to start over. I messed up, slacked off, and let me, you, and other people down. Give me the strength to stay committed. Give me a do-over. Amen.

#84 | Big Bang Experiment

In this experiment we will use a scaled-down version of the big bang theory in order to produce order and form out of chaos.

Items Needed

Watch—This should be a cheap watch, i.e., dollar store or less. [Health Warning: It will be detrimental to your health if you use one of your mom's extra watches.]

Tennis ball—This will be used to form a capsule. A tennis ball is optimal, but if one is not handy, you may use a ziplock bag, paper sack, or dirty sock. Just about anything will do.

Duct tape—For use of securing capsule.

Eye protection—Safety first. (You never know when someone might get an eye put out.)

Tools—I don't know exactly what tools will be needed, but every good experiment requires them.

Bonus optional tool—Hammer or other object that could be used like a hammer.

2 rolls [handwritten annotation pointing to Duct tape]

also used
- bunsen burner
- jet fuel
- fire extinguisher [handwritten annotation]

Objective

To create a watch from the mere pieces of a watch by using force and random alignment. Here's how:

Impact Force $= (M/t)*\{(1+c)*[(2/M)*(\text{Work})]^{1/2} - (r/d)*(cs_1 + s_2)\}$

Experiment Disadvantages

We cannot produce the same amount of force as would a collision of particles traveling at warp speed.

Experiment Advantages

We do not have to create life from lifeless materials as is the thought behind the big bang theory. We simply have to create a watch, functioning or not, from the basic parts of a watch. We are beginning from a much more advanced stage than the big bang theory starts from, so our experiment should be much simpler.

Setup

a. Dismantle watch as much as possible without breaking it. Remove wristbands, watch back, and batteries. Dismantle all internal parts.
b. Cut a hole in the tennis ball. Oh, that reminds me, scissors should be put on the list of tools.
c. Place watch parts inside the tennis ball.
d. Secure opening using duct tape, creating a capsule. (I would wrap the entire ball if were you, but hey, I'm an overachiever.)

Process

Take the capsule outside and locate a hard surface: brick wall, sidewalk, or tree, for example. While wearing your safety goggles, hurl the capsule at the hard surface with all your might. After impact, pick up the ball and shake. If it sounds as if a watch were created, then carefully open the capsule to reveal your findings. If, however, it still sounds as if there are multiple pieces of watch material in the capsule, then repeat the process. Shake well after each launch. Continue this process until watch is formed or you feel like a total idiot for believing it could happen.

Optional Hammer Step

If you feel that more force is needed, then place capsule on hard surface and hit capsule with hammer. Repeat, shaking for verification. [Death Warning: Do not use the dining room table or the floors inside your house for this process, or tomorrow you may wake up dead.]

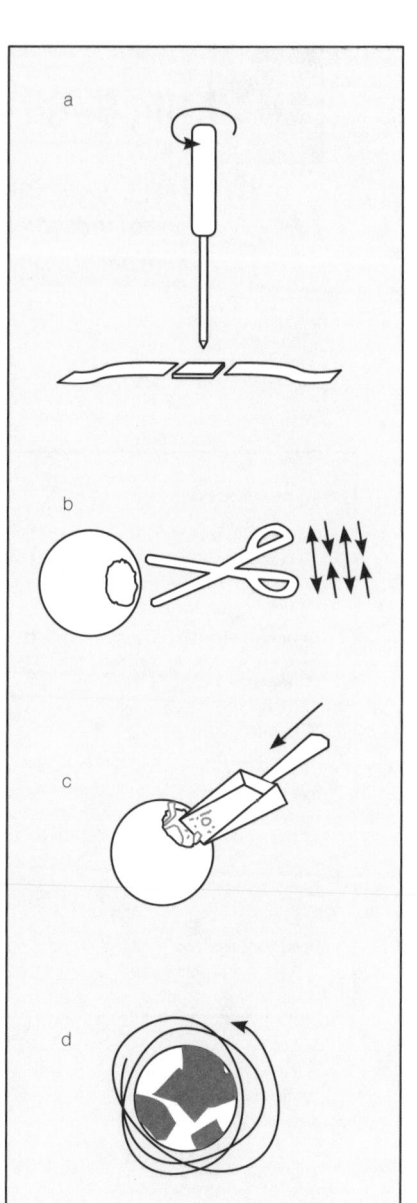

a

b

c

d

Small sledgehammer worked well

Conclusion

Even when using visible parts recognizable as those belonging to a watch, we still were incapable of hitting or striking with enough force or precision to facilitate an environment where even the basic theory of random alignment could create a watch.

Send results to Lab A.S.A.P.!

Application

Many people say they don't have enough faith to believe in a Creator. They believe in concrete science, and science points to a "big bang" as an explanation for the creation of the universe. Well, my little mad scientist, you just saw that you have to either have an insane amount of faith or simply be insane to believe that a collision of random particles in a random way with enough force will produce life from space dust. I don't have the kind of faith it takes to believe that space poo.

verse 2

For something to be created, there has to be something that can create. That means something bigger than luck, random alignment, and theory. Check out the story in Genesis 1. It says, "Now the earth was formless and empty." There was nothing here. And then a God who just speaks and things appear said, "Hey, turn on the lights." And there they were. (You should get the full meal deal in the first chapter of Genesis—just keep reading till you get to the end.)

If you are going to believe, believe in something bigger and more powerful than an accident. Put your faith in the Creator who did the creating. Choose to hope, dream, and wonder in the safety zone of the one who gives us our hopes and dreams. Otherwise, let me know how the watch thing turns out.

Your results:

_____

_____

_____

_____

Trust Me

Skydiving. I always thought it was a really cool thing done by really stupid people. Then I had to prove the theory right and go do it. Not only did I skydive, I went through the school that allows you to get certified to jump by yourself. And let me tell you, this whole process was the scariest thing I have ever done in my life.

Here are the basics. To jump solo you have to go through AFF. Don't worry about what that means (or see the Trust Me Glossary if you care about all these fancy-schmancy terms). Just understand that this is what the instruction course is called. I did my AFF at Skydive San Diego with two incredible jumpmasters, Brook and Katherine. In fact, Brook is there all the time, so if you want to go skydive, then go to www.skydivesandi ego.com and he'll hook you up or come check it at www.skydivedallas .com and tell them Lookadoo sent you (shameless plug for my skydive homies).

Warning: *Parachuting is a high-risk activity which may cause or result in serious injury or death. *Read and follow all warning labels, manuals, instructions, training or experience requirements and recommendations, and recognized parachute use procedures. *Parachutes sometimes malfunction even when they are properly designed, built, assembled, packed, maintained, and used. The results of such malfunctions are sometimes serious injury or death. *If you are not willing to accept the risks of sport parachuting, then you should reconsider your involvement in sport parachuting. *Any participation in parachuting is at your own risk, and you alone hold any and all liability for choosing to do such a crazy thing.

At Skydive San Diego the AFF program has seven levels. To get prepared, I spent the day with Katherine doing ground training to get me ready for the actual jumps. The next morning we left way too early in the morning to go out to Otay so we could hook up with Brook as soon as the DZ opened.

We went over a little more ground training, and the biggest thing that both of them kept telling me was that if you are unstable or in a bad spot, arch your back. That will solve just about every problem. You wanna stop flippin' around? Arch your back. You can't find your handle to pull? Arch your back. That is the number one thing.

The first two jumps were with both instructors. Brook was on my main side and Katherine on reserve side. They were giving me directions and making sure I was okay and that I knew how to pull that parachute. On jumps three, four, and five, it was just me and Brook. He jumped with me and stuck to me just in case, but one of my security blankets was gone.

Then came jumps six and seven. On these jumps I left the plane by myself, and I was supposed to perform several skills, and Brook wasn't supposed to touch me. Thinking about this all day really jacked me up. I followed my instructor around asking him question after question. "What if this?" "What if that?" Finally Brook stopped, looked me in the eye, and said, "Justin, just trust that what I am telling you works." He turned and left me standing there.

Crunch time was here. We boarded this plane and off we went, climbing to 14,000 feet. I didn't enjoy any of this ride. I was trying to remember everything I was supposed to do and when. I felt like telling Brook I couldn't do it and just quitting, knowing that I did five more jumps than most of the population of the world ever will. But I stepped up to the door, looked at my instructor, and out I went. Well, out most of me went. My body flew out while my ankle slammed against the door of the airplane, and my foot popped around facing inward and locked. This wasn't the first time this had happened to me, but this was the first time that it had happened two miles above the earth.

Not only did my ankle snap and lock but the hit threw me out of control. I was flipping and flopping, looking at the Earth from every possible position except the one I wanted to be in. I was losing altitude fast, and I didn't know what to do. This was it. The end. All of a sudden I heard Brook's voice in my head: "Trust that what I am telling you works." Ah, my salvation, my guide. I immediately arched my back with everything I had . . . and nothing happened. Now I was tumbling uncontrollably through the air *while* arching my back. I started thinking about what else might work, what I could do to get my world stable, because apparently he was wrong! But I had nothing. No other options, no other techniques, just faith that what Brook said works, so I kept arching.

Meanwhile, back in the plane, Brook was watching this fiasco. He told the pilot, "Well, it looks like this is the level I fail him on." He waited a couple of seconds and then said, "I guess I better go get him." He dove headfirst out of the plane, flying as fast as he could to get to me in time. He dropped to my level about the time I looked up and realized I was stable. A little party went off in my head: "It worked, it worked, it worked!" I went ahead and did what I was supposed to do in the air, pulled the parachute. The jerk of the parachute opening unlocked my ankle, it snapped back into place, and I landed right where I was supposed to.

As I gathered up my stuff, Brook came up to me smiling and laughing. He asked me what was going through my head when I was flipping around. I told him, "All I could think about was you telling me, 'Trust that what I am telling you works,' and I had no other choice."

That is when God kicked me right in the face. Immediately I could see him up there looking at us, his people, his children. We act all loving and committed to him and his Word. Then the moment something bad happens, we start looking for a new solution. We automatically think that he must be wrong or blind because his way isn't working, so we look for a backup to his directions. We want to take control of the situation and fix it. Or some of us just quit trying and ask, "Why would God do this to me?" And some people say that they are totally committed to Christ, but when life throws them into uncontrollable flips and chaos, they start running to other places for ideas to get them stable—Buddha, Mohammed, meditation, Kabala, anywhere they can look to get a new strategy or philosophy for their life. All the while God is watching us flail around and saying, "Trust that what I am telling you works. Trust that what I am telling you works."

Don't run off trying new philosophies, answers, or religions. Don't try to grab your world and control it by your own hands. When life comes at you full force, the only way to get stable is by sticking to the Word of God. Do what he is telling you. And guess what—at first, you may still be flipping outta control, but even then, trust that what God says works. Trust that his Son is the way, and you will get stable. It even says it in Deuteronomy 5:32–33, "So be careful to do what the LORD your God has commanded you; do not turn aside to the right or to the left. Walk in all the way that the LORD your God has commanded you, so that you may live and prosper and prolong your days in the land that you will possess." And in Proverbs 3:5–6, "Trust in the LORD with all your heart and lean not on your own understanding; in all your ways acknowledge him, and he will make your paths straight." Now that's what I'm talking about. If you throw yourself into the Word of God and trust him, then overcoming these whacked-out times of life that knock you around will give you the confidence that you can pull out of any situation that is thrown at you if you only "trust that what I am telling you works."

Trust Me Glossary

AFF: Accelerated Free Fall. An AFF student receives training on freefall jumps of 40 seconds or longer, accompanied by a qualified jumpmaster.

Jumpmaster: Someone who has successfully attended a USPA Jumpmaster Certification Course.

Ground training: Instruction and training on normal and emergency procedures, provided on the ground in a classroom-type setting.

Otay: Pronounced "o-tie." Common name used in the skydiving community to refer to Skydive San Diego because of its proximity to the Otay Valley.

DZ: Drop zone. Common slang for a skydiving center.

Instructor: Someone who has held a USPA jumpmaster rating for at least one year and has passed an Instructor Certification Course.

Main side: Refers to the side of the body closest to the main parachute handle.

Reserve side: Refers to the side of the body closest to the reserve parachute handle.

Me and this ol' cowboy horse trainer were chewing the fat one day. I don't know why, but that's just what cowboys do; they chew fat. He was telling me about a horse he worked with, and so I give the story to you.

"Brenda brought me a horse that had a problem that I had never heard of before. She explained that she would be riding along perfectly fine when all of a sudden the horse would slam on the brakes and start backing up. It didn't matter where they were or what they were doing. She was terrified. The horse didn't care what was behind them. It could be a highway, a gully, a fence—it didn't matter. And nothing Brenda could do could stop it. She would cluck, she would spur, she would use everything she could, but it would not stop the full steam reverse.

"I had never seen this before, so I loaded up the horse and took her to the arena. I saddled up and started through the tilled ground. We had warmed up to a trot when just like Brenda said, we stopped and started a full-throttle backpedal. I just held on and waited. We rounded the arena twice, *backward*. Finally the horse stopped, took a deep breath, and started forward again.

"After about five minutes of working in the pen, forward progress was again interrupted, and we went on our rewind voyage. Again I just sat on top and waited. And again we took a two-lap backward trip around the arena. After the second round, she stopped, took a deep breath, and we went on our merry little way.

"This happened three times. By the third time my friends had gathered on the top rail to watch the circus. One guy asked if this was my new barrel racing technique. Another fella shouted that he could turn my saddle around for me so I could see where I was going. All the while I just sat there, making backward rounds about the arena.

"We were going pretty good for a while and then, just like before, the horse stopped. I got ready for our little parade, but nothing happened. We stood there frozen. I could see her running the options in her head. We had done this three times. Six reverse laps around the arena. She took a deep breath, lowered her head, and continued our forward journey. From that moment on we did not have another backward marathon.

"Brenda came back at the end of a week, and I told her the horse was fine. She was so excited and questioned how I had made her stop going backward. I replied, 'We backed up a lot.' 'Wait a minute. Isn't that what she wanted to do?' she asked. 'Yep.'

"I explained to her that backing up a *little* seems like fun. But going two laps that way gets very uncomfortable. So I let the horse do it. Finally she would

REVERSE

I want to continually go this direction feeling this way, or do I wanna just go back in the right direction?

It may take a few times. We may be just like this horse and have to go several laps, several years, and several bad decisions going the wrong direction. But the Father is willing to wait on us to change our minds.

Yes, he could shorten the process and force us to go the right way. But in doing so, he would destroy our trust. We would resent him, and our spirits would be broken. He made us to be creatures of choice. He gives us the Holy Spirit in our lives to help us make the choice, even if that means making our lives very uncomfortable. Then he waits expectantly for us to choose to go back in the right direction. ●

get tired of it and go back to the right path. Sure, I could have beaten her into a forward motion, but I would have destroyed the trust and broken her spirit. So I let her have the choice."

See, sometimes God does that to us. Check it: Romans 1:24 says, "Therefore God gave them over in the sinful desires of their hearts." Basically, the people were walking backward away from God, and he said, "Go." But as Christians, when we "go," we really don't go alone. See, God has placed his Holy Spirit in our lives. When we keep wanting to go the wrong way, God may let us go. Pretty soon we will get very uncomfortable because the Spirit inside of us won't tolerate continued wrong living. So when God gives us over to what we want to do, it seems fun at first. But just like the horse thought backing up was fun, after a couple of laps of doing it wrong, we will have to make a decision: Do

Poor Skippy

Have you ever seen those cute little fishbowls with the plant sticking out of the top and the roots down in the water where little Skippy can swim through them? I like those. If I had a fish, I think that's the kind I would have.

And as a betta-fish-bonus, these things are low-maintenance. So low that I had three different people tell me that you didn't have to feed them because they got their nourishment from the roots. Now that's what I'm talkin' about. A little creature with a memory span of about four seconds plus no food required—I'm in.

I went to the pet store and I was going to get one of these perfect little aquatic wonder-worlds. I picked out the one I wanted and went to the head fish dude and said, "Hey, Mr. Fish Dude, what do I need to know about caring for this little fish dude?"

He went through all the water and cleaning stuff and how important it is to keep the cat away, and then he said, "And you need to feed him about four pellets every day."

He must have seen the confused look on my face when I stopped him and said, "Hey, hold up. What do you mean, feed it?"

"He's gotta eat," he said.

"Yeah, he eats the roots."

He looked at me like I was an idiot and said, "Ohhh, you're one of those."

"What do you mean one of those?" I popped back.

Mr. Fish Dude asked me, "Where'd you hear that? Your friends?"

Shameless book plug: Check out The Dirt on Drugs.

"Well, no. I heard it from three different people," I said confidently.

He said, "I don't care if you heard it from three thousand people. It's wrong." He went on to explain that people tell each other that their fish never has to be fed and it eats the roots. There are even a lot of people selling the fish on the side of the road who say the same thing. But it's all a total lie. The fish have to have food. But people think their little fishy is doing fine because they never feed it and he just keeps swimming around. The problem is, it could take up to six months for the fish to starve to death. So by the time little Skippy starts doing the backstroke, people think the fish got sick and died. They never figure out that they starved the little guy to death. You know what? They'll probably go get a replacement pet and starve it to death too.

Another shameless book plug: Check out The Dirt on Sex

How sad! I started thinking about all those fish out there hoping the cat will push over the bowl and eat them just to put them out of their misery.

I felt soooo stupid. I believed this fish tale just because I had more than one person tell me the same story.

I'll tell you something even crazier. I have people from all over the nation tell me that I'm wrong about ecstasy, marijuana, and alcohol. Like, "Marijuana is not addictive." "Drinking some alcohol is good for you." "X is really safe." And I ask them where they got their info. "Uh . . . a friend."

Or even sex. They tell me you can't get pregnant if you don't "finish." Or that you can't get a disease if you use condoms. And again I ask where they heard that . . . uh, my friends. Okay, fine, so someone on the same level as you with the same knowledge as you told you something and you believed it. Hmmm.

That's like going to the first day of ball practice with a new coach and asking your teammates what plays you're gonna run this year. Yeah, someone on the team will tell you, but guess what? They are making it up. They don't know any more than you do. So you'd better wait for someone to give you better knowledge. Someone who's been through it and studied what is really going on. Yeah, the coach, duh!

Hey, it's your life. But if I were you I'd get my info from someone a little more qualified than my buds. Get your goods from someone with the experience and knowledge to back up what they are saying. Like it says in Proverbs 13:20, "He who walks with the wise grows wise, but a companion of fools suffers harm." If you wanna get your life lessons from lame sources, it may take awhile, but slowly you might find out that you are just like little Skippy. Slowly dying because someone gave you a bad batch of info.

CAUTION: Be careful to not believe your friend just because they get a couple of right answers. A bud may know some truths about sex, drugs, or whatever, but don't make them your encyclopedia for life issues. Even the guy talking about what plays the team will run this year might get a couple right, but that doesn't mean he knows everything. It just means he made a couple of guesses that were right. Make sense?

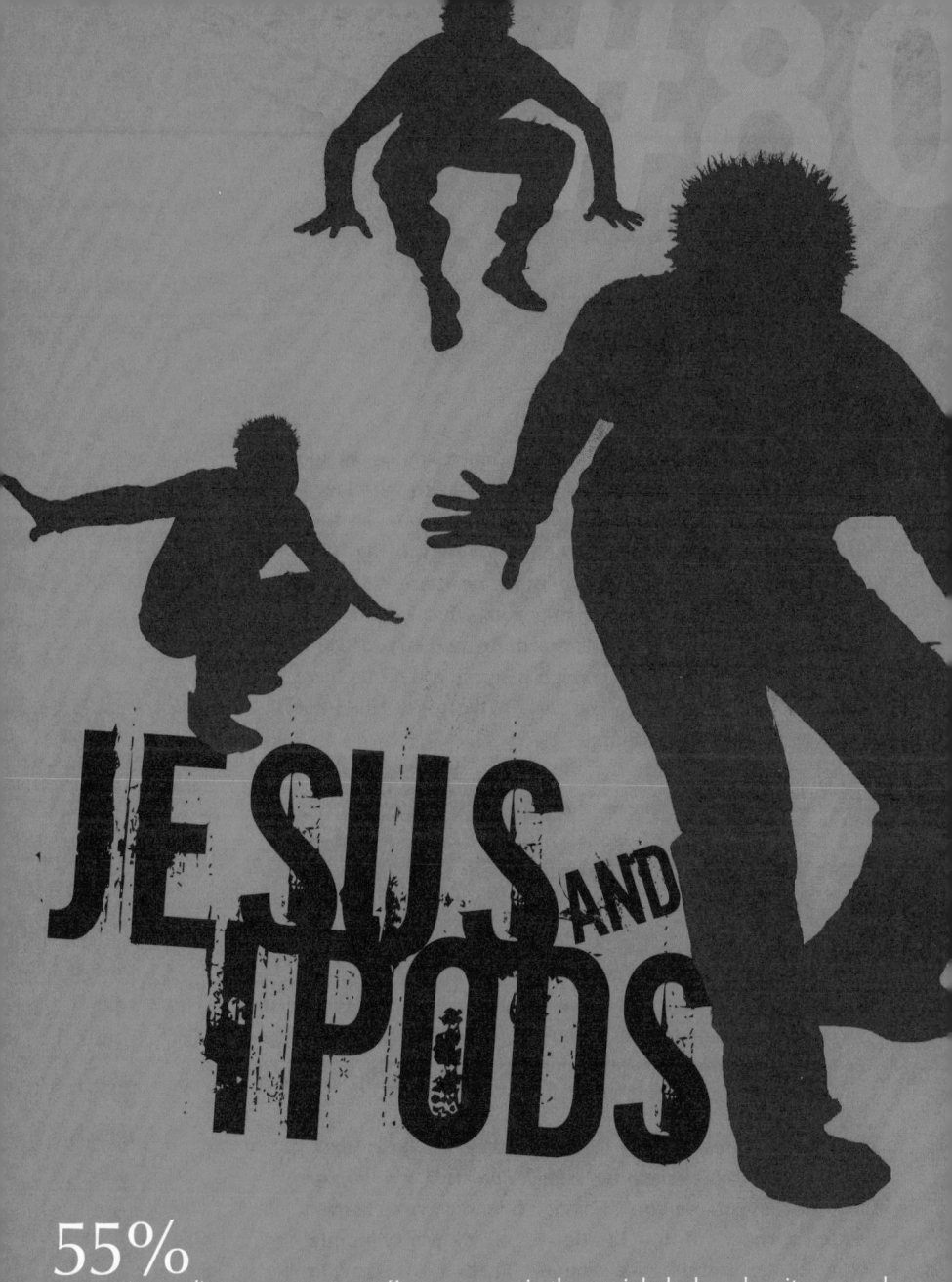

JESUS AND IPODS

55%

According to our sources [i.e., our cousin the social-phobe who sits around all day picking scabs and sending us useless information], in a poll conducted by Beliefnet.com, when asked what kind of music Jesus would have on his iPod, 55 percent said they didn't think Jesus would have an iPod.

Conduct your own poll. Ask your friends what they think Jesus would have on his iPod. If they give you the right answer, reward them by saying, "Peace be with you."

There you are. Day 1, minute 3.75 of your existence outside the maternal condo you've been chilling in for the last 9 months. You're cold, you're slimy, and you've never done anything to anyone. You're an empty vessel waiting to be filled with love and care. Then, outta nowhere, SMACK! Some child-abusing doctor spanks you. What kind of welcome party is this, and why is this dude mad at you? Does your mom not have good enough insurance? Did he have to leave his golf game to get here? What gives this idiot the right to slap you around?

By now you are 7 minutes old and you have learned one of your most valuable lessons...Life ain't fair. You will say those words many times throughout your life. "That's not fair." And guess what? You're right!

Your parents get a divorce—it's not fair. Grandma has cancer. It's not fair. The dude you like drops you for your sister. You get green beans caught in your braces and everyone calls you "booger-eater" for the rest of the year. It's not fair.

Forget fair for a sec. The bigger question is, "Is it just?" See, God created everything, right? The stuff we see and feel plus the stuff we don't. Gravity. Sound waves. He even created a system of how life flows, and it's pretty simple: "What comes around goes around." That's God. Okay, he didn't say it exactly like that, but he said it in a celestial merry-go-round kinda way when Paul popped off the letter he wrote to the Galatian people and said, "Do not be deceived: God cannot be mocked. A man reaps what he sows. The one who sows to please his sinful nature, from that nature will reap destruction; the one who sows to please the Spirit, from the Spirit will reap eternal life."

Margin Note: Galatians 6:7–8

Let me connect a few more dots here. All of us have let God down and blown it with him. And because of this we deserve death. Not just to fall over stiff but death of happiness, death of dreams, death of relationships. We live in a world full of sin. We do stuff to hurt God all the time. We don't mean to, but it happens.

See, when God set this world up, everything was cool. No pain, no death. It was just God and his creation. Sin jumped in the mix, and since that moment life isn't fair.

Random bad stuff seems to happen to good people, and some really cool stuff happens to some really horrible people. And you know what? None of us really deserves the good stuff. In the letter to the Romans Paul breaks it down like this: "All have sinned and fall short of the glory of God." We don't deserve the bonuses God gives us. Check out what it says in the very next verse, "and are justified freely by his grace though the redemption that came by Christ Jesus." You don't hear people griping about that.

No one says, my grandmother came home from the hospital. It's not fair. My family lived through a horrible car wreck. It's not fair. My dad got a raise. It's just not fair. Yeah, it has nothing to do with being fair. It's all about grace, justice, and God's creation.

Life ain't fair.

God is just.

Rom 3:23

Stand-In Girlfriend

Starring Brooke Wilson

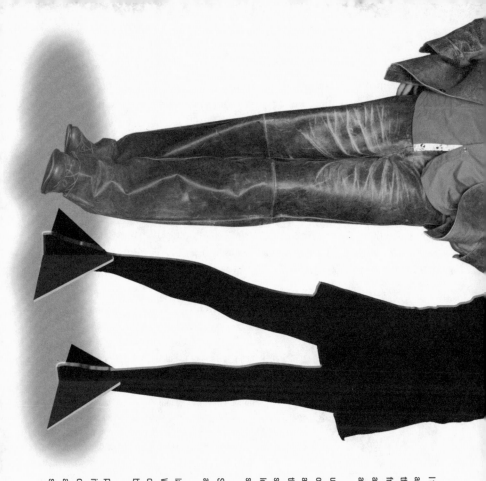

I finally figured out what was going on. I had been wondering why my best guy friends always seemed to be calling more, hanging out more, and text messaging me random thoughts more at certain times. Then I thought about what made those times different from the times that they were more "distracted" and I didn't see them or talk to them as much. That's when I figured it out. I was most important when they weren't dating anyone. I was the Stand-In Girlfriend.

In plays and on movie sets there are lead roles, the supporting cast, extras, and even understudies. The lead role is the focus of the story; the supporting cast is there to help or hinder the lead in their story. Extras are faceless people who fill in the background, and understudies know every line the lead has in case something should happen to them. If the lead cannot perform, the understudy saves the day. But what about the stand-in? Stand-ins are just used to see if the blocking is right, or if the camera shot looks good. Heck, even stunt men and women have a more glamorous role! But the stand-in is just a space filler, a warm body until the important actors are used.

That was me with my guy friends. When they weren't dating anyone, I was the Stand-In Girlfriend who made sure the blocking worked or that the camera angle got a good shot.

It was almost like they were just trying to stay in practice until their next leading lady came along. We'd talk on the phone all the time, go see movies, go to dinners. We would go on non-dates constantly. And then as soon as some gorgeous girl was cast in the lead and was ready for her lines, the Stand-In Girlfriend was sent to the back of the room until she was needed again.

I'm sure many of you girls and guys know exactly what I'm talking about and have played the role of Stand-In Girlfriend or Stand-In Boyfriend countless times. But I say it's time to get a bigger role. We're better than our name being lost in the scrolling credits. We are lead actors and actresses, every one of us. We just have to believe that and be ready for our lines when the right costar comes along. Don't be a stand-in in someone else's movie; be the star of your own movie.

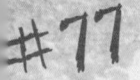

Have you ever felt like this huge cloud is following you around? It's like it is following you everywhere and you can't shake it. You seem to get away from it for a minute, or maybe you're just distracted from it, but it comes right back and covers you with the blahs all over again.

I've been feeling like that for three days now. It's like this dark cloud won't leave me alone. I am talking about a *real* cloud. Not just feeling depressed but a real life cloud.

See, I was leaving Dallas. I got on the plane and then sat on the runway cramped up in the little seat, feeling like a baby in a papoose pouch, not able to take off because of a storm. This cloud, this funk, was all around us. Finally we took off and I flew to Arkansas. And guess what? The storm that kept us from getting off the ground in Dallas met me in Arkansas. That night was crazy. Rain, hail, tornadoes . . . welcome to Arkansas. It moved on past us, I went and spoke in my schools, and everything was pretty much okay.

I hopped on another plane and headed to Savannah, Georgia, and guess what we got to fly through? The same storm that I had already seen twice. Strap in tight and hold on, because the airplane rodeo was starting. We bounced up and down, side to side . . . yee-haw!

I landed in Savannah and drove about an hour out to the beach. I was there about thirty minutes, just long enough for my old friend to catch up with me. The same storm that caught me in Dallas, Arkansas, and somewhere over Mississippi was now hanging out with me at the beach. I just couldn't get away from it.

Have you ever felt like that? This funk is all around you. You are down and blah and you don't really know why or how it started. I get like that quite a bit. And when I do get down, all the wannabe psychoanalysts come out and try to explain why I'm like that and what I need to do. So let me be like one of those friends and hit you with a little holy psychobabble and maybe give you some blues clues and bummer busters.

1. Sin. Lots of times when I'm in the blah zone, it's because I'm doing something that is blocking my vibe with God. Do a sinventory of your life and check to see if there is anything that could be keeping you disconnected, especially if it's a repeat of a repeat kinda thing. Are you gossiping and talking trash about other girls? Looking at porn? Lying to the parentals? Making fun of kids at school? Ask God to show you if you have any of that stuff and he will. "Search me, O God, and know my heart; test me and know my anxious thoughts. See if there is any offensive way in me, and lead me in the way everlasting" (Psalm 139:23–24).

2. Test. All of this could be just a big test. Check in with Job. You talk about some major cloud coverage. He lost his land, his wealth, his family, and even his friends were turning on him, and it was all a test. Not some sick, twisted quiz to see if he passed. It was a test to prove that Satan had no power to break down a man who was totally committed to God and that anything the Enemy could destroy, the all-powerful God could restore bigger and better. All of this could be a test of your reactions and commitment. So don't freak out in the middle of your funk. It could be a test to show Satan and others that you've got what it takes.

3. Listen Up. Sometimes I get all blahed out because God wants to chat and he knows that he needs me to slow down and get secluded enough so I will hang loose and listen. Check yourself. Do you seem to be somehow "getting away from it all" but not in a negative way? Then you may want to start listening. God may be trying to talk.

4. Hormone Zone. Yes, this could be a major reason. Hormone changes can totally whack out everything you thought you knew. If it happens frequently, then track your emo-cycle for three months. This will let you know if there is a pattern. Hey, this is for the fellas too, not just the sheilas. Watch and see if this is a one-off issue or a cycle that you need to get some help with.

5. 'Tis the Season. There is a lot to be said for the cliche, "It's just a season you're in." 'Cause you know what? It might be true. Our entire existence is set up to go through seasons. Change. Ups and downs. Rain and drought. Sometimes you just have to keep pressing on and understand that this season will change just like the last.

Well, I don't know if that did anything for you, but when you start hitting one of those pouty periods, come back and reread today. The blahs are not something to be afraid of or to run from. They should tell you that something is about to happen. Something new and different. Learn to read your blahs and it will totally change the time from just being depressed to a time when you get to become more like the person God has called you to be.

BLAH Ha Ha Ha Ha Ha

Compassion without **ACTION** is Dead

Compassion. We all *should* have it and everyone says that they *do* have it, but I don't know if we really understand what that word means.

See, we attach a heavy emotional price to compassion. The more something rips at our heartstrings, the more compassion we think we must have. I really don't think that's right. It just means you feel really bad about something. You know what I'm talking about. You see some starving child on TV or you hear stories about some tragedy, and you have this emotional outpouring and call it compassion.

The Scripture says, "Faith without works is dead" (James 2:26 NASB). You know, it's the exact same way with compassion. Compassion without works is dead. If you say you have compassion and you don't do anything, then you just feel bad for someone. And that really doesn't mean much.

Like if someone talks about you behind your back, and then they come to you saying how sorry they are and that they won't ever do it again. You could sit there and say that you have compassion on them, but if you do not forgive them, well, you're a fake. If you see someone in the street who is hungry and lost and you say, "Wow, I feel so much compassion for them," but you don't do anything to help, then you don't know what compassion really means.

Here, do this: The next time something happens and you have an emotional reaction where you really feel bad for someone or someone's situation, don't say you have compassion. Instead ask yourself, "What about this sitch is making me feel bad?" Then ask, "What could I do to help?" It could be anything. It doesn't have to be some huge media-worthy contribution, but what part can you play? Then do it.

Compassion is not an emotion; it's an action. It's okay to feel for people, but in doing something you will actually have compassion. Make this a habit. Every time you feel deeply, ask yourself those questions and do what you can, and you will become a person of compassion.

75 Jessica

"That's not what's sexy about me

[referring to her 'provocative style'].

I believe that my soul and my faith

are what's sexy about me.

It's all about what's inside."

—Jessica Simpson

Uh, okay . . .

Check it:

Do I believe beauty comes from a connection with God? Yes. Do I believe that in some cosmic God-fashion, people become more attractive the stronger they are spiritually? Yep. But this is a supernatural, unexplainable beauty that is totally connected to the Creator of beauty. When you show up flashing your biz to everyone, it's easy to explain where the hotness comes from. It comes from the skin you're in and how much of it you're showing.

So don't let this get confusing for you. You know how you've heard "beauty is only skin deep"? It's true—when talking about that explainable attractiveness that can be pegged by your flesh. But the hotness that comes with getting totally filled with a relationship with Jesus, a beauty which will only get more intense the more intense your connection with Christ is—that beauty will last forever. Focus on forever. Don't get all wrapped up in the wardrobe woes and beauty blues. Live for the true beauty. Connect with God on a personal, consistent level and your hotness will go all the way to the core.

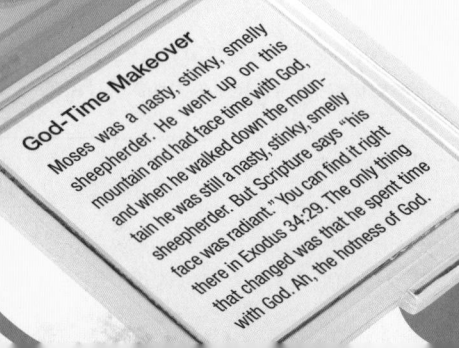

God-Time Makeover

Moses was a nasty, stinky, smelly sheepherder. He went up on this mountain and had face time with God, and when he walked down the mountain he was still a nasty, stinky, smelly sheepherder. But Scripture says "his face was radiant." You can find it right there in Exodus 34:29. The only thing that changed was that he spent time with God. Ah, the hotness of God.

Show 'Em My Motto

Today you get to discover your life motto. This isn't some cheese-filled deal that means nothing . . . oh, it could be that, but it could also really help you in how you live your life.

See, if you have a motto for your existence, then that becomes the standard that gauges what you do and do not do. It makes your decisions really easy. If it connects with your motto, you go for it. If not, you change channels.

If you already have a motto that you live by, rock on! If not, here's the how-to:

1. Choices. Get a list of as many quotes, thoughts, and ideas as you can. It can be movie quotes, lines from songs, verses from the Word, thoughts you have had. It doesn't matter where they come from. Anything that inspires or motivates you. Write down as many as you can think of.

When jotting some words down, here were some of mine.

- If you are not content where you are, then don't try to get more
- Live with no regrets
- Every man dies, but not every man truly lives
- He who pursues righteousness and love finds life, prosperity, and honor
- What we do on earth echoes in eternity

Let's see, I had one book quote, two movie lines, a mom line, and a Scripture. Just random stuff.

2. The Decision. Here's what you do now. Imagine yourself as an old person, sitting on the front porch and thinking about your life. Then think through each of the finalists that you have scribed, asking, "Would I be upset if I missed my mark on this one more than any of the others?" If the answer's no, take it off your list. Do this over and over. When you get down to one, you've got it!

Write your new motto on everything. Your notebook. Postcards. Make it your signature on your emails. Put it on your sites. This will become your automatic guide in how you run your life.

Every once in a while, go back and see if your motto is still the same or if your vibe has changed.

My life motto ended up being "Live with no regrets." I would totally hate it if I slacked on this one more than any other. So this has become a guiding force for me. When I have a decision to make I ask myself, "What would I regret more? *Doing* this or *not* doing it?" And whichever one I would regret the most, there's my answer.

Justin Lookadoo

Listen to my fave song!

Here is a cool true story that I'm thinking about putting in my new book *97*. Let me know what you think!

The stud-muffin of the school started calling this girl. *Of course* she was interested, so she did the girly thing and went into detective mode, getting the dirt on all his history, his crushes, and what happened with those girls. She arranged "accidental" meetings between her friends and his so they could dig up info. Everything checked out, so she turned on her girlness. Yeah, he was hooked.

Sure enough, he called and asked her out, and she said, "Sure." As it was getting close to date night he called to chat with her, and then he asked her, "So what do you wanna do Friday?" She was kinda like, "Huh?" but she went with it and said, "Let's do dinner and a movie." She figured it was safe.

He said, "Naw, I don't want to do that, what else you got?"

She said, "Well, what is something you can think of?" She had already read *Dateable*, so she knew that he needed some help being a man.

"No, I asked you. Give me something else."

"Noooo," she said. "This is the way it works. I gave a suggestion and you didn't like it. Now you give a suggestion." (He was too stupid to realize *any* suggestion would have been perfect with her.)

"I don't care how it works. That's not the way I run my dates."

She snapped back, "Apparently you're not man enough to run your dates. You make the girls do it. Well, I'm not a man, and I'm not dating a dude who can't be one either." Click.

Schaweeeeeet! Yeah, word got around with a quickness on this one. The guy got hounded and the girl got crowned. It wasn't all glam though. A lot of dudes stopped chatting her up. And some of the dudes who were jockeying for position to go out with her dropped it like it was hot. Why? Because they were the same as the other guy. They made the girls do all the work, and now they knew they didn't have a chance. So there were fewer left for her to choose from, but they were all solid choices.

Listen, girls, a guy will put time and money into what he thinks is important. If basketball is important, time and money. If his car is important, time and money. If you are important, time and money. If he is not willing to come up with a plan and figure out how to fund it, you are not that important.

There are going to be some guys you have to train. They really do want to go out with you, but no one else has ever allowed them or even expected them to act like a man. So it may be a little slow at first. But once he gets the hang of it, he will be taking the lead and will be a man, and you, ladies, can relax and be the girl guys want to chase after and win.

10/9/2006
Wow. Glad I read this before calling my date.

10/10/2006
Dude   who in the world does your hair!!!

Never Saw

He was in the best spot in his life he had ever been. He was jet-setting around the country with his job. He had a nice place, a fast car, and cool toys. He was on top of his game. He did what he wanted when he wanted and how he wanted. And it was good. He was loving his life, and he was definitely not looking for any chica to come in and mess with his mojo.

She had been very successful. She owned her own company and her own house, her perfect life was set up . . . until her dad got sick and went into the hospital. Of all the kids, she was the one who dropped everything to move back home and deal with the chaos.

She would take care of her dad during the day, but she needed cash. She still had major bills coming from the life she'd left, and it got overwhelming trying to live in two places. So she got a job waiting tables at night. She was older than the others there, but it was good money and she needed the work.

She was in the worst spot of her life. She lost her house. She lost her business. She was sleeping on her mother's couch because she had no other place to go, driving a beat-up, borrowed pickup, and waiting tables at a local joint. She was not looking for a man. In fact, she hoped none would see her.

It Coming

In steps God.

He arranges for this successful, content, on-top-of-his-game fella who was not looking for a girl to walk into the restaurant and meet a homeless, alone, can't-seem-to-find-the-game waitress who was not looking to attract a man.

He ate. They laughed. She talked. Still neither looking, wanting, nor expecting anything more.

As time went on, he ate at that restaurant so much he tried everything on the menu. She always managed to take her break when he would come in . . . after taking his order, of course.

Time passed. Conversations deepened. Connections were made. And on November 26, 2004, an out-of-place waitress married an unexpecting businessman, and they became Justin and Emily Lookadoo.

Ahhhh! Yeah, that's my baby. And did you see the theme here? We didn't do it. God did. We sure as heck weren't Easter-egg-hunting for a mate. We were living what the psalmist says in chapter 37, verse 7: "Be still before the LORD and wait patiently for him."

You want to know how to hook a lifelong hottie? Stop looking. I know, it doesn't make sense [kinda like the platypus—see #86], and it's even harder to do. People told me this too, and I thought they were idiots just like you think I am. But trust me. It works. You can date. You can have friends. But don't put so much pressure on making sure the next one is the one. Back off and wait for God to do his deal. And then you will be able to find the one that God made specifically for you. ●

There I was, a junior in high school, playing varsity basketball and thinking I was a stud . . . I mean, I was a stud. Anyway, this was the hyped game of the season against our biggest rival. Not only that, but I had twenty people in the stands just to watch me play. Friends, family, people from church, even my girlfriend from another school—they all were at the game for me.

We were going through our warm-up drill getting psyched up. We were at home and I wanted to get the crowd really going. So I took the ball, dribbled three times and took a huge leap and I launched myself toward the goal. I cocked the ball behind my head, and as I flew by the goal, I slammed the ball into the rim. The crowd went crazy. I grabbed ahold of the rim and my feet kept swinging because of

the momentum. About the time my feet swung level with my head, my hands slipped off the basketball rim and I went flying through the air, did a flip, and landed flat on my stomach. My chin bounced off the floor, busting it wide open. Blood went everywhere. I reached over to pick up the ball and couldn't even hold the ball in my hand. I was hurtin'.

I left the gym followed by my twenty fans and went straight to the hospital. By the time it was over, my little stunt had awarded me eight stitches in my chin, a broken right wrist, and a cracked left one.

I had six weeks of sitting out to think about what had happened. And yeah, I found many reasons for the fiasco, like being stupid, but the basic issue was that I held on too long. If

#71 Let It GO

God can't give you something new if your hands are full of the old.

I would have let go quicker, my feet would have been in the perfect spot, and I would have nailed it. But I held on to the rim too long, and that got me way out of the safe zone.

That's what happens with God sometimes. We have a superman grip on something we think God wants us to let go of, but we don't want to. So we hang on to it too long, and it ends up crashing around us and breaking our heart even more.

Maybe you've hung around with some friends almost your entire life, but they've been getting into stuff you're not cool with and you feel God is wanting you to let go of them. But you've been pals forever so you are holding on . . . too long.

It could be something you're doing. It could be video games. It could be something you keep thinking. I don't know, but you do. Something that God is trying to get you to let go of. And if you hold on to it too long, it will destroy you.

Like when the prophet Jeremiah told King Zedekiah that he needed to surrender. He needed to let go of what he had and God would protect him and he would be okay. But that didn't make much sense to the king, so he just ignored God and kept hanging on to what he had. Check out the crash that happened when he lost his grip. "There at Riblah the king of Babylon slaughtered the sons of Zedekiah before his eyes and also killed all the nobles of Judah. Then he put out Zedekiah's eyes and bound him with bronze shackles to take him to Babylon." Yeah, letting go would have been a lot easier after all.

It might even be some cool stuff that God wants you to let go of. Maybe you have been teaching a kids' group at church and you think God wants you to give it up. It may be a person, it may be a hobby or a habit, and for some reason you feel like God is saying, "Let it go." Then do it. It doesn't matter if it doesn't make sense to you right now or what will happen next—just stop hanging on and let it go. If you keep a death grip on it, sure you will keep it for a few more ticks. But once you are totally out of balance with God's plan, your grip will slip and your world will crash hard. ◀

Jeremiah 39:6-7

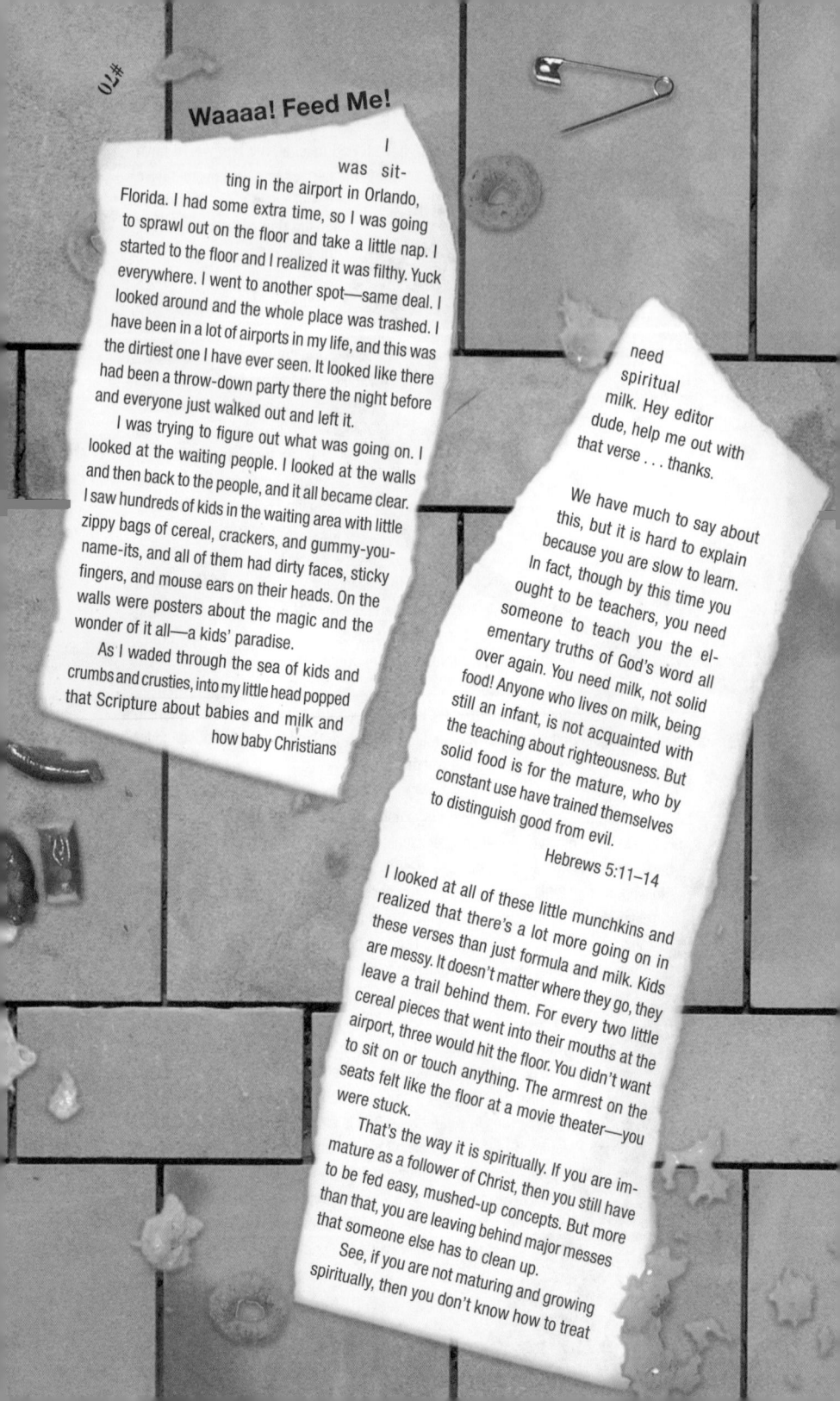

Waaaa! Feed Me!

I was sitting in the airport in Orlando, Florida. I had some extra time, so I was going to sprawl out on the floor and take a little nap. I started to the floor and I realized it was filthy. Yuck everywhere. I went to another spot—same deal. I looked around and the whole place was trashed. I have been in a lot of airports in my life, and this was the dirtiest one I have ever seen. It looked like there had been a throw-down party there the night before and everyone just walked out and left it.

I was trying to figure out what was going on. I looked at the waiting people. I looked at the walls and then back to the people, and it all became clear. I saw hundreds of kids in the waiting area with little zippy bags of cereal, crackers, and gummy-you-name-its, and all of them had dirty faces, sticky fingers, and mouse ears on their heads. On the walls were posters about the magic and the wonder of it all—a kids' paradise.

As I waded through the sea of kids and crumbs and crusties, into my little head popped that Scripture about babies and milk and how baby Christians need spiritual milk. Hey editor dude, help me out with that verse . . . thanks.

We have much to say about this, but it is hard to explain because you are slow to learn. In fact, though by this time you ought to be teachers, you need someone to teach you the elementary truths of God's word all over again. You need milk, not solid food! Anyone who lives on milk, being still an infant, is not acquainted with the teaching about righteousness. But solid food is for the mature, who by constant use have trained themselves to distinguish good from evil.

Hebrews 5:11–14

I looked at all of these little munchkins and realized that there's a lot more going on in these verses than just formula and milk. Kids are messy. It doesn't matter where they go, they leave a trail behind them. For every two little cereal pieces that went into their mouths at the airport, three would hit the floor. You didn't want to sit on or touch anything. The armrest on the seats felt like the floor at a movie theater—you were stuck.

That's the way it is spiritually. If you are immature as a follower of Christ, then you still have to be fed easy, mushed-up concepts. But more than that, you are leaving behind major messes that someone else has to clean up.

See, if you are not maturing and growing spiritually, then you don't know how to treat

other people exactly how
God wants you to. You will do things
that you think are okay but totally go against God.
You can't understand what God is saying a lot of
the time because he uses big-boy words that you
don't understand yet. You need to grow up.

How do you know if you are growing? Here's
an easy Q: How long have you been a follower of
Christ? Let's say four years. (You pick your own
number and do this for yourself.) What if there
was a four-year-old still downing mama's milk and
slurping down pureed peas? Yeah, that's a little
freaky. Well, if you are a four-year-old believer, do
you still count on someone else to read the Bible for
you, chew it up for you, and tell you what it means—
and even that only happens once a week?

Here, do this. Down below write several ways
that you can tell you have matured physically.
Things you can do or understand, whatever. I'll
even help you get the little squirrels going in your
brain. Stuff like, "I can walk. I can chew. I can run."
Just jot several down. Go!

Now, right below it write down several things
that prove that you are maturing spiritually. Stuff like,
"I have six verses memorized. I have read through
all of Romans and understood it." Go!

If you have a gigantic list on the second round,
then rock on and keep rocking! If you had some
trouble, then you may wanna get off the faith
formula, ditch your baby talk prayers, and start
growing into a spiritually mature giant.

Don't know how? Here are some thoughts.
Get your buds together from your church or
youth group and all do the list thingy you just

did. Have everyone
come up with all the
proof that they have ma-
tured physically. Then list the
things that prove they have grown
spiritually. For most groups that
will be a shorter list.

Then show this to your
youth leaders and tell them
that you want to get off the formula and start eating some biblical buffets. Tell them that you want
them to lead you through a book like
*Step Off: The Hardest 30 Days of Your
Life.* It's a 30-day adventure guide that
will supercharge your spiritual life, and in
the end you will see some major growth
and be able to add more proof to your
spiritual list.

Get a plan together. What books will
you read? Verses to memorize? How are you
going to amp up your prayer life? Don't just
sit there and think you will grow spiritually
without a spiritual plan.

*Book Alert. You will probably not
be able to find enough books in the
store for your entire group. So go
to www.lookadoo.com and tell us
what you need, and we will get you
and your youth workers hooked up.*

Do You Know?

the air speed velocity of an unladen Swallow?

Have you ever heard of this dude named Rob Grotheer from outside of Savannah? What about his wife Gayle? How about Tommy and Christa Green? Or Tom and Elizabeth Shook? Well, have you heard of Paul and Wez Childers?

I know, random questions, random people. And it's okay if you don't know them, because they probably don't know you either. But every person that I just mentioned has impacted your life. If you are reading this book *hello!* or listening to someone read this book, then you are being affected by those people.

Why? you should ask out loud inquisitively, especially if you are in a quiet place. Be-

cause they are the reason this book was written.

Here's how it works. This book had to be written, but I couldn't stay at home and do it because Emily is there. And she is a little bit of a distraction ... okay, a lot. We would much rather hang out with each other than write a book. So we were looking for a place for me to go hide and write. It had to be quiet and have nature, a city somewhat close by, and someone we know just in case we needed them. We thought of Rob. We called him and asked if he knew of anything, and he started working his magic. He said, "I couldn't find you one location but I found four. We'll just move you when we need to."

Not only did this group of givers let me use their homes, but Rob gave me his Jeep for the month and they stocked the houses with food. All of this adds up to the words you have in your hands. If not for these people that you've never met, you wouldn't have this book.

That is exactly the way *you* are. Your decisions have major impacts on people you'll never know. It doesn't matter if you believe it's true or not, because it is. Let me show you how this could play out.

There's a kid at school who never talks to anyone. He's sitting alone at lunch *again*, but today you go sit with him and talk. He doesn't show any emotion, but inside he is doing cartwheels. On his way home he sees the stray dog that he throws rocks at every day. But today he pulls out some food he smuggled out of the cafeteria. The dog follows him home, and the kid adopts him. Meanwhile, his grandfather is very old and alone. The boy decides to give the dog to his grandfather so he won't be alone all the time. This gives his grandfather a renewed excitement for life.

Look. Your one conversation had a profound impact on a kid, a dog, and a grandfather. Don't look at me like, "That won't happen." It does happen. You just may not ever get to see the impact. The people I listed at the beginning will never know the impact they had on you either . . . but it happened. No *you* make it happen.

I dare you to

Try writing an entry that combines Les Mis and a shark bite.

y
people.
    Why? yo
loud inquisi
if you are in a q

Les Misérables

"Your misery will be your ministry."
—Bishop T. D. Jakes

Ever played the scar game? You know, you start flashing your flawed flesh and give the story about how it happened.

Yeah, I got this one skateboarding when I was nine.

I got this one falling off the house.

This is where I got stabbed.

Oh yeah? I got bit by a shark. [I had a kid do that to me in Virginia as he showed me his thrashed leg. He won.]

Scars are cool. Now, the process of getting a scar sucks because there is pain involved. But each scar tells a story. And when you see someone with a fresh wound, you feel for them because you know exactly what they're going through.

That's life. You may end up going through some hellacious stuff. Maybe you already are and it sucks. And once you get through it, whatever it is, you will have some scars. These scars will be the things that you get to tell other people about so that you can help them. And when you see someone else wounded like you were, you will be able to reach out to them like only someone with your scars can.

"Your misery will be your ministry."

And the God of all grace, who called you to his eternal glory in Christ, after you have suffered a little while, will himself restore you and make you strong, firm and steadfast.

1 Peter 5:10

No Hablo Espan-Girl

Guys and girls speak totally different languages. Yeah, we use the same words, but the internal dictionary that we each have that places meanings on those words . . . totally different.

Girls, people are telling you all the time that guys will lie to you. Heck, I tell you that all the time. And a lot of them will. But there's a bigger problem, and that is the differences in the way we talk and listen. So I am going to change everything.

Let me be the one to say this to you, ladies . . . guys *don't* lie to you. When they tell you something, they mean it. They just don't mean it like you take it. When a guys says, "You make me feel different than anyone else in this world," he means it. He just doesn't mean it like you take it. Ladies, you think he said that because you are soul mates. No, that's not what's going on. See, guys are logical thinkers, and in his mind it's true. You are different than Kara, so you will make him feel different than she does. And Erika is different from you and Kara, so she will make him feel different.

When a guy says "I love you," he means it. He just doesn't mean it like you take it. It's not that you are the only one for him, forsaking all others . . . nooooo, that's not what he said. When a dude says "I love you," ladies, it's true, he loves you. And what he means is, "I love my dog. I love my car. I love a number three supersized. And oh yeah, baby, I love you too." This isn't a pyramid with you on the top, then the car and the dog, and then the number three. Nope, you're all on the same level. With time and God, your status in the lineup will change. But remember that what he is saying and what you are hearing are different things.

TODAY, LISTEN TO PEOPLE TALK. SEE IF YOU CAN START RECOGNIZING THE THINGS THAT GUYS SAY AND WHAT GIRLS HEAR. IT WILL BE HARD AT FIRST; AFTER ALL, IT'S A DIFFERENT LANGUAGE. PRETTY SOON YOU WILL HAVE IT DOWN, AND YOU WILL BE ABLE TO COMMUNICATE WITHOUT SETTING YOURSELF UP FOR HEARTBREAK.

Are you caught up in the coffee craze? It's insane! A cup of coffee costs more than airplane fuel. It totally makes me mad. I am even more miffed that I still lay down the cash for these little caffeinated creations.

Q: Are you a coldie or a hottie? Coffee preferencely speaking, that is. Do you go for the hot cappuccino or the cold crappuccino? Yeah, I know, I meant to say that. I like mine hot!

People are loyal to their climate. Not too many are equal opportunity coffee drinkers. It's pretty much one extreme or the other.

Have you ever grabbed that cup of joe and taken a big gulp only to dis-

#66

Coldie or Hottie

cover that it was at room temperature? Omigosh, I hate that. I start looking for the trash, a plant, somebody's shoe, anywhere I can spit it. That's got to be the worst. I like my coffee hot. If I have to, cold. Room temp isn't even on the menu!

This is the same thing God was saying in the book of Revelation. In the third chapter, verses 15 and 16, it says, "I know your deeds, that you are neither cold nor hot. I wish you were either one or the other! So because you are lukewarm—neither hot nor cold—I am about to spit you out of my mouth." How would you like to be the one God wants to spew out? Not a good place to be.

That is exactly where you are if you say you are a Christian and then go off and live like you don't even know anything about Christ. Listen, get in or get out. If you say you are a follower, then go full-on living for Christ. Be hot. But if you say you are and are showing you're not, then you make God sick. In fact, you are hurting his cause more than anyone. Even the people who are not believers and don't claim to be are more pleasant than those faking it. Get in or get out. Get hot or cold. Lukewarm makes God puke.

You can't show that! What are you thinking!

LOUNGER WAS THE COOLEST CAT EVER. He was a street cat. Grey and white, thin and spunky. He adopted me when I was at home after a road trip.

I had seen him around the apartments before, but we never were tight. He didn't really get too close to anyone. I was cleaning up my place one day and ran outside to throw some stuff in the trash, and when I came back I found Lounger sprawled out in the middle of my bed. He looked pretty comfy, so I threw some food in a bowl for him and finished what I was doing. I left the door open in case he wanted to leave . . . and he never did.

We hung out together for a couple of weeks until it was time for me to leave again. So we said our good-byes. I said, "I'll see you in two weeks." He replied, "Meow," and we parted ways.

When I came home I parked the car, and on my way up the stairs to my apartment I whistled, and Lounger came running up with me. This became our life. We'd hang out for a few days, then we'd both hit

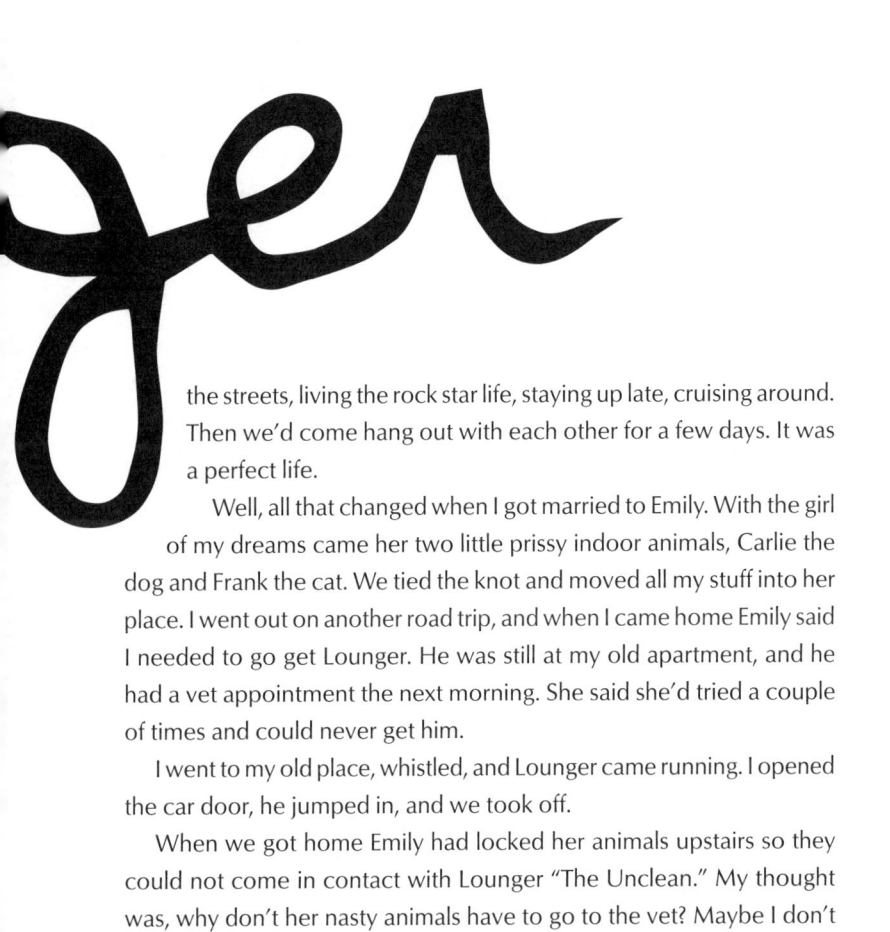

the streets, living the rock star life, staying up late, cruising around. Then we'd come hang out with each other for a few days. It was a perfect life.

Well, all that changed when I got married to Emily. With the girl of my dreams came her two little prissy indoor animals, Carlie the dog and Frank the cat. We tied the knot and moved all my stuff into her place. I went out on another road trip, and when I came home Emily said I needed to go get Lounger. He was still at my old apartment, and he had a vet appointment the next morning. She said she'd tried a couple of times and could never get him.

I went to my old place, whistled, and Lounger came running. I opened the car door, he jumped in, and we took off.

When we got home Emily had locked her animals upstairs so they could not come in contact with Lounger "The Unclean." My thought was, why don't her nasty animals have to go to the vet? Maybe I don't want their sissiness rubbing off on my Lounger. Not a battle I would ever win, so I didn't even try.

Emily had made fish for dinner, and she gave Lounger a little piece of the skin. Then she gave Lounger his first bath. It went pretty well. He didn't like it, but he didn't freak out. And then she put his first little collar around his neck. Emily had stayed up late the night before making it. It had a little cut-out kitty face with his name on it. Ahhh, so cute.

It was getting late and I had been on the road for a while, so it was time for me to crash. I was logging some serious sleep time when all of a sudden I had four paws land right in the middle of my chest. I opened my eyes and I was face-to-face with this furry little creature. See, Lounger was still on street time. It was 2:00 a.m. and he was ready to play. I threw him off, rolled over, and in about two minutes he was standing on the back of my head. I jumped up, put Lounger in the closet, slammed the door, and told him that he could come out after his appointment.

The next day Emily took Lounger to the vet and then came back and got me. She said the vet wanted to talk to us. We went into the office, and the vet said that something didn't seem right, so they ran some tests and found that Lounger had feline leukemia, and we had a choice to make. We could take Lounger home and let him die a slow, horrible death, meanwhile infecting our other cat and putting him through the same thing, or we could put Lounger down.

Wait a minute. I didn't come here for this. I came for some shots, clip the nails, stick a thermometer up his butt, and we'd go home happily ever after. I didn't sign up for this.

We made our decision, and they brought Lounger back into the room. We played and talked for about half an hour, I kissed him and said, "Good-bye," and they came and took him away. I took the collar that Emily had made him off his neck and put it in my pocket, and we left.

As we were driving home I took the collar out and started crying. Emily asked me what was up, and I said, "**I wish I would have known**. I wish I would have known that last night was our last night together. I would have been up playing. I wouldn't have thrown him in the closet. I would have stayed up all night with the little feather and string thing."

She began to cry and said, "I would have given him the whole slab of fish."

I slipped the collar on my wrist and told Emily, "I never want to be in a position where I have to say 'I wish I would have known.'"

I wear my Lounger bracelet all the time now. It reminds me to live my life with no regrets.

"I wish I would have known this was the last thing I would say to my mom. I wouldn't have yelled at her when I left."

"I wish I would have known that the loner, kind of dorky kid at school was thinking about suicide because he was so lonely. I would have tried to talk with him."

"I wish I would have known that pushing my girlfriend to go too far would send her searching to fill the void for love in her life by jumping from guy to guy."

"I wish I would have known."

You know what? You can have this reminder too. Emily and I have had so many requests for a Lounger bracelet that we started making them just like she did the first one. Each one has a cat face with "Lounger" written on it and "I wish I would have known." And each tag is made specifically so that it will fade away. With time, with water, with just living life, the face will fade. This is to remind us that things never stay the same and that we should always be on the lookout for ways to help others or to say something nice. Like it says in Hebrews 3:13, "encourage one another daily, as long as it is called Today," so we never have to say, "I wish I would have known."

If you want to order a Lounger bracelet for you or for your group, then catch up with us at www.lookadoo.com. We'd love to get them to you.

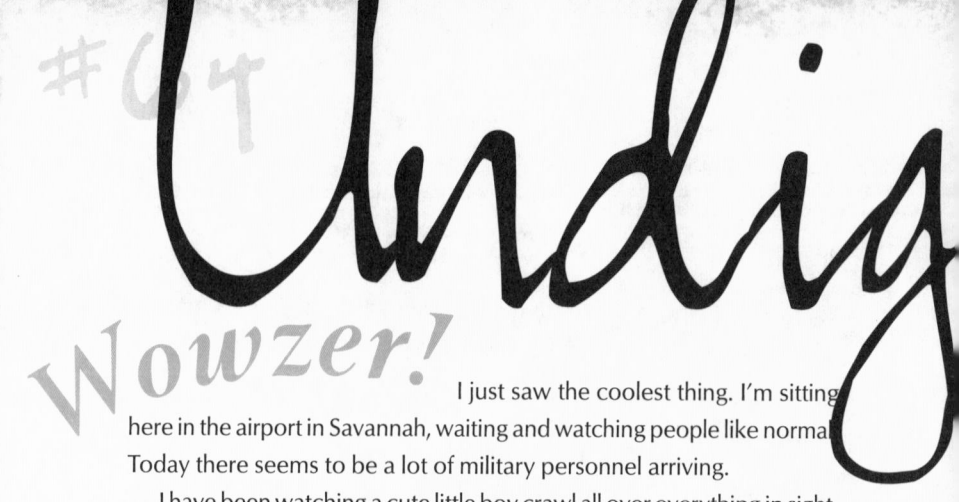

Undig

Wowzer!

I just saw the coolest thing. I'm sitting here in the airport in Savannah, waiting and watching people like normal. Today there seems to be a lot of military personnel arriving.

I have been watching a cute little boy crawl all over everything in sight. His mom is all dressed up, sitting quietly and looking a little nervous. All of a sudden everything about her changed. Her eyes lit up, and she shouted at the little boy to look. He turned, shrieked, did a little dance, and then took off running.

I looked behind me and saw a guy with a military haircut and standard issue backpack sprinting toward us. He dropped everything he was carrying on the ground just in time for the boy to fly through the air and tackle him. They were rolling around on the floor, and when his wife got there, she pounced on top of both of them. Now all three were rolling around, stuff scattered everywhere, causing a scene.

It was totally undignified. It was sloppy. It was raw. It was real. And they didn't care what anyone thought. They were in the moment and nothing else mattered.

What a cool visual. That is what

was happening with David when he was praising God and some people thought he was not being dignified enough. And check out his response in 2 Samuel 6:21–22, "I will celebrate before the Lord. I will become even more undignified than this, and I will be humiliated in my own eyes." I love that confidence and that attitude. "I'm going to be so in the moment, so in the zone, that I don't give a rip what you think. Stare, laugh, crack jokes. Think I'm weird. I'm gonna do it anyway."

That is exactly how we're supposed to be when we are connecting with the Creator. Why is it that we think our worship must be dignified,

nified

structured, appropriate? We should be running up and throwing ourselves into God's arms.

What's the blocker? What keeps us from being totally in the moment? Are you embarrassed? Afraid of what others will think? Don't want to cause a scene? Have never had permission? Well, now you do.

I GIVE YOU TOTAL PERMISSION TO LOSE CONTROL.

Get in the moment, and if you feel a little weird or inappropriate, just remember David—a king, a warrior, a man of authority and dignity, and he got downright "undignified" when he praised God.

PERMISSION SLIP

The holder of this pass is entitled to totally undignified behavior while praising God. Coupon may be used or combined with other offers. Value is doubled where prohibited.

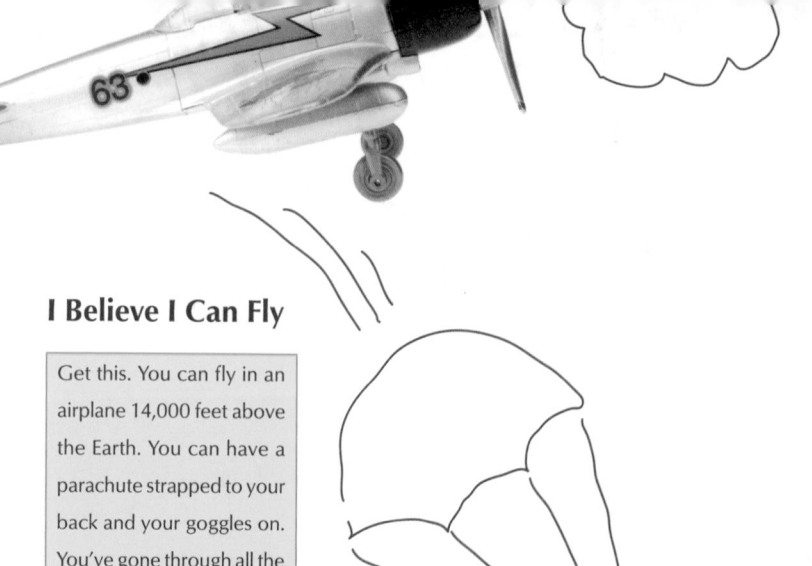

I Believe I Can Fly

Get this. You can fly in an airplane 14,000 feet above the Earth. You can have a parachute strapped to your back and your goggles on. You've gone through all the instruction, you know what to do, and you have all the faith in the world that this is going to work. But even with all of that, if you stay in the plane, you've got a dead faith. In fact, the letter James wrote said it flat out: "Faith by itself, if it is not accompanied by action, is dead." You gotta get out of the plane. Without that, you've got no faith.

James 2:17

Hey, if you just live your life, you go to church and play it safe, you don't really risk anything, then you have no faith. It's dead. You have to get out of your comfort zone. You've gotta try things that are going to totally freak you out at first. God wants you to go big. And you'll never go nuclear if you can't conquer a little firecracker.

Soon to be hitting a fair amount of resistance.

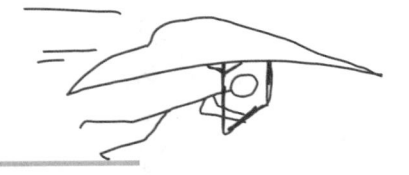

So what does this mean to you in your world? I don't know. It's different for everyone. For you, maybe you would never get up in front of someone and tell them something cool God has done for you. Then that's a good place to start. For me, that's a no-brainer. I'll do that without a prob. But I hate writing. It's a horrible process for me. But here I am stepping way out of my comfort zone and clicking away at the words.

God helps me draw stick people.

Cool.

If you need some help on this one, grab your buds, your youth worker, or maybe a teacher you're cool with and come up with a whole list of stuff, from talking to someone you don't know to going on a mission trip in the jungle with no electricity or plumbing. Start small and keep growing.

a really thick brick wall

I heard it said once that the mind is like a parachute—it only works when it's open. Yeah, that's beautiful to say, but it's crap. You can stand out in your driveway and open up a parachute; that doesn't mean it's working. Nope, a parachute only works *when it hits resistance*. Faith is the same way. It only works when it hits resistance. Push through things that you would normally resist, and watch your faith increase with the resistance.

#62 Relational Flossing

You are sitting in the dentist's chair, lying back with a death grip on the arms, and this person with a mask on has both hands shoved completely in your mouth and is scraping your teeth with a chainsaw. And all of a sudden they pull back and points to the poster with the lover of bicuspids and molars ask you The Question. "Have you been flossing?"

Your first instinct—lie. But then you think, No, they can tell. But you can't just say no, so you stammer out, "Uh, yeah, some." And this person with a mask on and the caption, "Only floss those you want to keep."

It's wild how just a little bit of leftovers stuck between your teeth can eventually destroy them. And if you don't get it out of there pretty quick, the stuff will start to harden, and then it takes some major work to fix.

That's the way it is with our relationships too. If we do something to hurt our friends and we don't clear it up pretty quick, it will start to destroy the relationship. Resentment, hurt feelings, and anger start building up to the point that it will take some major work and damage control to repair what you had.

Don't let it wait. Constantly give your relationship a checkup and make sure there's nothing hiding in the cracks. Remember, a quick floss of "I'm sorry" is a lot better than trying to salvage a rotten relationship.

#61

8 Seconds

Get a timer, a clock, a watch, anything that you can watch for eight seconds. If you're at all technical and you can set it to count backward and beep after eight seconds, then do that. If not, just grab something you can watch for eight ticks.

Whenever you are ready, just sit there and experience the time passing for eight seconds. Go. Eight seconds. That's nothing. It just blew by without you even noticing it. Now do this. Go and find a two-thousand-pound bull that is bred to destroy you, is meaner than Brad Pitt is to the paparazzi, and wants nothing more than to slam you to the ground and stick his hoof through your spleen. Strap yourself on its back, and then hang on for eight seconds. Yeah, those few ticks just became a loooooong time.

Obvious Question Guy has to ask, "How can the same amount of time blow by *and* feel like an eternity?" Obvious Answer Guy says, "Perspective." The way you are looking at a situation will determine how you feel about it. And how you feel about it will determine how you act in it. You never know how someone else is seeing the exact same situation.

That is why we should be so careful not to judge the way someone acts in a given situation. You may think they are overreacting or being a drama-mama, and maybe they are. But you don't know that. Cut 'em some slack. Remember, what you see as no big deal, they may see as earth-shattering. You really don't know what is happening in their head or behind closed doors. Give them a break, and maybe they will do the same for you when you freak out about something that seems small to them.

You, therefore, have no excuse, you who pass judgment on someone else, for at whatever point you judge the other, you are condemning yourself, because you who pass judgment do the same things.

Romans 2:1

RUNNING FROM RAIN

BY BROOKE

I was on the phone with Justin the other day and he just started laughing out of nowhere. I had to stop to think if I had just said something funny. Hmm . . . nope. I had to know what was so hilarious, so I asked, "What's going on?" And he explained. "Oh, Brooke, get this. I'm sitting near the beach and I just saw this woman who was in her bathing suit, standing in the water. It just started raining, and when she felt the rain she started running for cover. She didn't want to get wet! Get it?"

I have to admit, the visual of a woman standing in water running because she didn't want to get wet from the rain seemed pretty funny and stupid. But then I realized something: I see people do that all the time. Okay, so they're not actually at the beach and it doesn't start raining, but it's a metaphor, so give me a break.

Do you have friends who are waist deep in sin? At one time they were dry and standing on the beach looking at the dark water, and then they decided to take that first step in. And then another, and another, until they were gradually waist deep in the waters with the shore long behind them. Sin creeps up on you that way. You take one step, and then another, and then another . . . until you're in the waters too. By the time you're that deep, you don't even remember that first step that froze your toes.

Then the rain comes down. Sometimes it takes being thumped on the head for people to realize their situation. This woman realized as the rain thumped her head that she didn't really want to get wet, so she ran back to the shore. When you or your friends finally get hit over the head with it and realize that you're surrounded by sin and don't want to be there, run back to the shore. Get out of the water and towel off. No one gets dry instantly, but eventually we can all get dry and stay that way.

"Should you not fear me?" declares the LORD. "Should you not tremble in my presence? I made the sand a boundary for the sea, an everlasting barrier it cannot cross. The **waves** may roll, but they cannot prevail; they may roar, but they cannot cross it."

Jeremiah 5:22

Do you get wetter running in rain or walking?

Answer: I think Yes.

#59

CHRISTIAN = ADEQUATE

> Whatever you do, work at it with all your heart, as working for the Lord, not for men, since you know that you will receive an inheritance from the Lord as a reward. It is the Lord Christ you are serving.
>
> —Colossians 3:23–24

Do you think Christians are afraid of stuff being over-the-top good? I mean, not you personally, but I'm talking the Christian kingdom as a big group. Do you think that if something pushes the limits of creativity, then Christians think there must be something wrong with it and it must not be godly? I'm just asking.

I was hanging out with this guy who was a film major at one of the top arts academies in the nation, and he also happened to be a Christian. He said it was an interesting study of the Christian psyche that as soon as you saw a clip hit the screen, you could tell it was going to be a Christian deal. Not because it was beyond the creativity

and excellence of the others, he said, but because it had this vibe of being *almost* really good. The lighting was *almost* right. The effects were *almost* perfect and the script was *almost* intriguing, but . . . not quite there.

What about this? What do you think when I put the word *Christian* in front of anything? Not what *should* you think but what do you really think?

How about "Christian school"? What do you think? Most people lean toward stuff like private, Bible-based, good education, college prep, some pretty good stuff.

What about if I introduce you to a group and I tell you they are a Christian band? Is your first instinct, "Wow! These guys must be some of the best musicians in the world"? Or is there a hint of "Oh, they must not be that great"? A brief thought of "Well, they'll never be able to compete with Coldplay"? Don't feel bad if you lean more toward the negatives. That has been the status quo—"Oh, you couldn't make it as a regular band, but you are a great Christian band."

Heck, what about a Christian speaker? Is your first thought, "Hold on, because he's about to rock my face off"? Or do you just kind of sit there waiting for the same-looking dude to get up there and say the same-sounding speech so you can sit there sportin' the same kind of bore- dom. I know the an- swer to this one. I am the speaker dude, and I see your faces when I get onstage.

What about this? What if I said "Japa- nese carmaker"—what would pop into your mind? Dependable. Long lasting. The best.

What if I said it was a "Christian carmaker"? Would you automatically think the same stuff? Probably not.

Where have we missed out? When did we become so accept- ing of stuff that is almost good? The apostle Paul wrote a letter to the Colossian people and told them they needed to quit slackin' and "Whatever you do, work at it with all your heart, as working for the Lord, not for men."

Yes, as Christians, we should be accepting. We should be loving and encouraging, but we should be **EXCELLENT**. That means not everyone needs to sing a solo at church. Not everyone needs to teach. Not everyone needs to produce movies. There are lots of bands who are Christians out there changing the status quo. They are not looking to be the best "Christian" band. They want to be the best, period. Same with speakers, writers, painters, producers, and actors. It's time we stop grading what is good on a curve and start striv- ing for excellence. Work to be the best, period! So today, tomorrow, and the rest of your life don't just accept stuff that's average because it's Christian. Be the best because you are a Christian.

I heard a dude say one time that he believed that God gave the idea of MTV to many dif- ferent Christians, but no one would take the risk and do it. But it was a great idea, so somebody finally took it and ran with it.

Colossians 3:23

RUDE PEOPLE

You just can't be nice to some people. You try and you try, and you're the one getting beat up for trying to be nice . . . sheesh.

Let's see if we can get down to what's really going on. Okay, there's this kid at school that everyone pretty much ignores. The only time someone talks to him is to push him around or to make fun of him. This happens pretty much every day. You decide you are going to make a difference, so you walk up to the kid and you are syrupy sweet. You want to show him what nice looks like, so you speak to him and he rips you apart. He yells, talks trash, and says some really mean stuff.

Mental this. What if there is a dog tied in a yard and every day kids come by and throw rocks at it and kick it and then just take off running? This happens every day. The more it goes on, the madder the dog gets. You feel bad for the dog, and you decide to do something about it. So the next day you walk straight up to the dog, and you are being as sweet as you can be. You even have a treat in your hand. What's the dog gonna do? Yep, he will try to rip your face off.

Would you just walk off thinking, *Man, that dog is a jerk. No wonder people throw rocks at it*? No way. You have watched what happened to this dog. It started out nice but then got beat down so much that it snaps at anyone who gets close. If you are really going to make a difference, you have to keep coming back and back and back. You have to let the dog know that you are not like everyone else and you are not going anywhere. You will have to take the barking and the abuse, but if you just be there and be consistent, in his own time this dog will start getting closer and closer to you until you guys become best buds.

And something else. I have had all kinds of animals. The ones that have been strays—the rejects, the ones that reacted the worst at first—they are the best, most loyal friends. They

← Beware of rude people in trash cans!

> "LET US NOT BECOME WEARY IN DOING GOOD,
> FOR AT THE PROPER TIME WE WILL REAP A
> HARVEST IF WE DO NOT GIVE UP. THEREFORE,
> AS WE HAVE OPPORTUNITY, LET US DO GOOD TO
> ALL PEOPLE, ESPECIALLY TO THOSE WHO
> BELONG TO THE FAMILY OF BELIEVERS."
>
> GALATIANS 6:9–10

would never leave me or try to hurt me, but if you tried to, watch out! They would protect me at all costs. Because I am the one that reached out and meant it.

Rewind. Go back to the kid at school. Are you connecting the dots yet? This isn't rocket surgery. This is easy dot-to-dot action. That kid at school will probably attack you, and it doesn't matter how nice you are. Every person who has ever gotten close has hurt him, so he is in a defend-and-destroy mode. And you know what? If you walk away like, "No wonder you don't have any friends" and you never try again, you just became like everyone else.

If you really want to reach out to people, then get ready for the abuse. Get ready for the anger and the lashing out, and just sit there and take it. They are not yelling at you; they are railing against every person who has ever hurt them. Take it!

With time, with consistency, with knowing that you are not going to turn your back on them, they will slowly start softening. They will lose some of the edginess, and eventually they will let down their guard.

The big bonus is that this person will probably be one of your best, most loyal friends. They will never leave you and would never do anything to hurt you, and if someone else tried . . . watch out. Because you are the one that reached out to them and meant it.

Guys Better Step Up

One of my best friends has a daughter who is super-yum-delight. She's tall, beautiful, athletic, intelligent, not psycho, and has an incredible relationship with Jesus. She is a dude's dream girl. So of course she has had guys chasing her around her whole life . . . uh, not so much. In fact, she never had anyone ask her out. She went her entire high school career sitting at home with the parents every Friday and Saturday night. Hey, I love my folks, but they are not the excitement I want to relive every Monday morning when everyone asks, "Whaddya do this weekend?"

She stuck it out and people lied to her all the time and said, "Oh, there are so many good guys out there." *News flash* No, there aren't. And then they would say, "Just wait until you get to college; there will be so many more guys to choose from." True. And there will also be so many more losers.

When she went to college, guess what she did every Friday and Saturday? Yep, sat at home. Yeah, she had some guys ask her out, but they didn't get too far because she refused to lower who she was. Physically, intellectually, spiritually, emotionally, socially, she had it all together, and she wouldn't lower her standards just so that a guy would seem like he had it all together.

In January this dude asked her out. And man was he . . . whoa! He was tall, almost 6 foot 4. Built! Not some steroid ranger, but he had a great bod. He was smart, like pre-law major smart. He had a solid fam. He was in a Bible study. He was the package! Oh, and guess what else he was, ladies? No, not gay . . . RICH. Hottie!

Well, he asked her out and she said no. I was like, you gotta be joking. Hey, I'm secure in my manhood and *I* would go out with this dude.

She said he had just broken up with his girlfriend, and she wasn't going to be the rebound. Hey, that's cool. But he really wanted to go out with her and asked when he *could* ask her out. She said, "Hmmm . . . May."

Stupid! No dude is going to wait until May.

May 1 came around and she got a phone call. He said, "You said I could ask you out in May. It's May, and I want to go out with you." This time she said yes! A year later they had a fairy-tale wedding complete with white horses, a chariot, and dancing under the stars [insert collective sigh from every girl reading this book].

A lot of you are even sitting there going, "Omigosh, I want that to be me." Listen ladies, it can be. This isn't some fictitious story that only happens in fantasy land. It can be you. But girls, hear me loud. I'll even put it in bold letters for you. **Never, ever lower yourself so that a guy seems like he's better than he really is.** This is an epidemic in our culture. Girls, you try to tone down your good stuff. You become *not* so beautiful. *Not* so smart. *Not* so spiritual. *Not* so . . . whatever. And you do it so that today's slacker guys don't feel intimidated, like you are out of their league. Face it, girls, you *ARE* out of their league.

That's what was happening in Joshua 23:7–8. The Israelites were in the middle of a bunch of people who didn't live up to their standards—to God's standards. And Joshua told them, "Do not associate with these nations that remain among you; do not invoke the names of their gods or swear by them. You must not serve them or bow down to them. But you are to hold fast to the Lord your God, as you have until now." Do not compromise.

It will be hard. I'm not gonna lie and say that it won't. But don't lower yourself to someone else's level so they appear to be a better fit. You make them step up to yours. And you know what, if you stay solid and keep growing physically, intellectually, spiritually, emotionally, and socially, there will be a lot fewer guys to choose from . . . and all of them will be a lot better choices.

Ahhh

1-999-STP-UPPP • 1234 Lookadoo Lane, Dateable, CA, 90210

The Oldies

What do you call your grandmother? Granny? Grams? Ga-ga? Write it over there. What about your grandfather? What do you call him? Write it there too.

Have you ever gotten stuck behind some little old lady who can barely see over the steering wheel and she's flying at about 17 mph in a 55? You're running late, and she has planted herself right in the middle of the lane so you can't go around her, and there's nothing you can do.

What do you say about her? What kind of stuff do you start yelling?

Have you ever gone into a store for a quick grab and you get in line behind the old dude who puts his stuff on the counter and every time the cashier says something he says, "Huh?" so the cashier has to keep repeating everything?

How about when you sit down beside the elderly couple at church or a school play? The man has his pants hiked up all the way to his armpits and his pants don't match his jacket, and don't even get me started on the white tube socks. Meanwhile, she has lipstick smeared all over her face. She's got on earrings that look like fishing lures, and they both smell, well, like old people.

What kind of jokes do you and your friends start cracking? Do you make fun of them or get frustrated with them?

Well, you know that old lady in the car, the old man in the store, and the elderly couple—yeah, those are someone's grandparents. Think about whatever names you might have called them, because someone else calls them (insert the name you call yours). That is someone's MeMaw. That is someone's Paw-Paw.

This hit me when I was in 10th grade. I was riding with my mom through the town I grew up in, and all of a sudden she did a *Dukes of Hazzard* power lock 180 and headed the other direction. Once I got my heart kick-started, she drove up over the curb, and I knew she had lost her mind. I looked out the window

ahold of it with one hand, and he was using the other one to help rock himself back and forth.

She looked at me and said, "Get out and help that man." I gave her a "C'mon, do I have to?" look, and she shot back a "Don't make me kill you" look.

I got out and the man was pretty freaked. He had fallen and he couldn't get turned around enough to crawl up the fence to his feet. He said he had been trying for about 15 or 20 minutes.

I helped him up and let him hold on to my arm, and we walked all the way back to his house. I was soooo embarrassed. We were walking along the busiest street in town, and several people I knew went by honking and shouting out the window.

Once I got the man home, I hopped back in the car and slumped way down, hoping no one else would see me.

Mom said, "Thank you."

I said, "Yeah."

Then she looked at me with a tear in her eye and said, "That was somebody's Pa." That's what we called her dad. "What if it was your Pa on the ground and nobody stopped to help?"

Smack! Right between the eyes.

The next day I went to school, and I gotta tell you, I didn't realize how many people saw me helping that man. And they all thought it was way cool. I became like this little mini-celeb because of it.

Listen, be patient and take the time to talk to the old people. God laid it down pretty straight in Leviticus 19:3. "Rise in the presence of the aged, show respect for the elderly and revere your God. I am the LORD." So if you don't want to tick God off, then take care of the old people. Besides, they really do have some cool stories. And remember, you're going to get to where they are right now.

How Would You Like It?

"Do to others as you would have them do to you."

Luke 6:31

How would you like to have you as a student? Think about it. Think about the way you act in class. How do you act with your teachers? Are you rude? Do you talk all class? Do you just sit there and stare at the wall? Are you always cutting up and never have your homework? How would you like to be *your* teacher?

How would you like to have you as a child? Are you disrespectful? Do you do what your parents ask? Do you ever say stuff like "I hate you"? Are you always getting into trouble? Do you help around the house without being threatened? How would you like to have to be *your* parent?

How would you like to have you as an employee? Can your boss count on you? Are you lazy? A slacker? Always late? Do you look for ways to help even when the uppers aren't around watching? How would you like to have to work with you?

How would you like to have you as a friend? Are you friends-till-the-end loyal? Will you do anything for them? Do you tell their business to other friends? Do you ignore them if they make you mad? Do you talk about them behind their backs? How would you like it if all your friends did the same stuff you do?

How would you like it if you were that girl who is on the fringe of your "inner circle"? Do you let her hang out with you guys when you need something and then ignore her at school?

Or what if you were mad at a girl—how would you like to be the girl you were mad at? Would you forgive her and just move on? Would you make snide cracks about her just loud enough so she could hear that you were talking about her? How would you like to be that girl and get treated the way you treat her?

How would you like to be the father of the girl you are hooking up with? Do you treat her as a gift, a child of God? Do you push her to do things with you physically? Do your hands touch her in places that you wouldn't touch your grandma? What would you do if your daughter wanted to date a guy like you? ▪

How would you like to be the God of you? Would you think, "Yeah, I am proud of him"? Or would you be like, "I watched my Son get tortured and slaughtered for her?" Would you think, "He's not even trying. He's wasting my time!" Or would you be so proud because of all the time you spent hanging out together? Would you, as God, look down at you and think, "She gets it. My Son died for her, and it was worth it." What would it be like if you were the God of you?

Don't just blow by these questions like a race car blows by a three-toothed redneck. Stop and think about it. And wherever you thought, "Aww, dude," that is where you need to change. Grab ahold of those issues and figure out how to do things differently. Become the person that when you look at you, you'll think, "Yeah, I'm doing it right." •

Today I've got nothing for you. Instead, we're going to check in with God and see what he has.

Do this. Close your eyes and clear your mind the best you can. Not yet—wait until you read everything. I'll tell you when to go.

Tell God, "God, I am here. Whatever you want in my head, make me think about it now."

Then jot down whatever hits your membrane. For some of you it will be like a machine gun firing at you. Thoughts will hit you faster than you can write. Some of you will sit there and you will wait . . . and sit . . . and wait. There may be only one thing. That's perfect too. Whenever anything comes up in your brain file, ask God, "What about it?" Write down whatever he throws at you—and then do it.

A friend of yours may pop up on your mental screen. Ask, "What do you want me to do?" He might come back with, "Pray." If so, pray for them even if you don't know why. You may get, "Call." If so, give them a shout and say, "Hey,

I just wanted to give you a call and check on you." Hey, this may end up being for no other reason than to make you smile. And that's okay. God wants you to smile.

You may have an issue you have been hiding and trying to ignore. Porn. Cheating. Lying. If it pops up in your brain, ask God what he wants to show you or tell you or what he wants you to do.

That's pretty much it. It's all on you. Remember to write it down. You'll be amazed. And for those who need a little recap here ya go.

1. Clear your mind.
2. Ask God to fill it.
3. What does he want you to do with whatever hits your mind?
4. Do it.
5. Make sure to write it all down.

Oh, before you go, you may want to try this again tomorrow. And maybe give it a shot the next day too. And then maybe the next. But watch out, before you know it you'll be doing what they call "prayer."

go!

Give Yourself a Hand

Grab a pen and draw a picture of your hand right here.

Come on, play with me. Get a pen and draw.   ↓

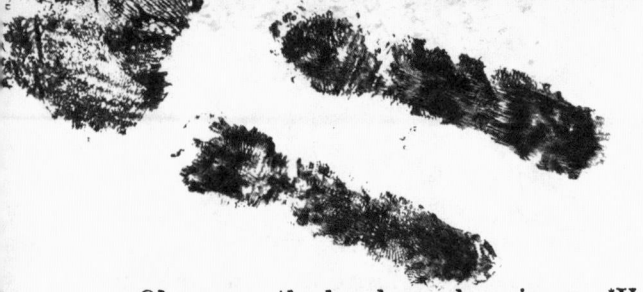

Okay, now the hand you drew is *you*. *Hello, you.* And being *you*, the psycho-head-doctor people tell us, you are made up of five main areas: physical, intellectual, spiritual, emotional, and social.

Think about you, the real you, and see which one is your strongest area. Whichever one it is you are going to write it on the thumb of the hand you.

For you it may be obvious. If you hit the gym three hours a day, you count every protein, carb, and fat, and working out is your life, then you pretty much know that physical is going on your thumb. If that's not you, then figure out which one is your strongest area. Take as long as you need to. The hand you drew will wait.

Now, after you have gotten your thumb, analyze and figure out what your #2 is. Are you more a social butterfly than a bookworm? Write this one on your index finger.

Go to #3. Out of those you have left—physical, intellectual, spiritual, emotional, social—which is your third strongest area? Write it on your middle finger.

You can guess what to do now, right? Decide which is the next strongest and scribe it on your ring finger.

Then figure out which is your fifth strongest and put it on your pinkie. If you have to think too much on this one, you may want to make it the intellectual one. (Aww, the pinkie people!)

There you have it. You in a handprint. Here's what you are going to do next. Take whatever you put on your pinkie and write it down here:

_____

You are going to figure out how to make that your thumb.

See, if physical was the number five, then get a plan together and work it until it's number one. Start slow and go bigger. Get to the gym. Start working out. Get some of those videos to give you buns of pure granite and exercise at home. Take a foodventory and change the way you eat. Don't know how? Then go to a gym or a YMCA and tell them you're not ready to join a club yet, you just need someone to help you get started. Someone will help you. If not there, find someone who is into fitness and ask them what to do. People are always asking Emily (remember my loud-mouthed, skydiving, WEIGHT-LIFTING wife) to help them at the gym. She is a fitness queen and always willing to help. That's the way most of the physical folks are. So get help and keep working at it until it is #1.

Once the little pinkie becomes #1 then you have to redraw your hand. They've all shifted one finger. Now, without changing anything else you are doing in the other areas, figure out how to make the new pinkie #1. If it's spiritual, then get going and make a spiritual plan that will get it to be your strongest area. Do what it takes. Buy books to read. Get a group together. Talk to pastors. Youth pastors. Anyone who is spiritually huge. There are some intense helps out there to heat up your walk. When you have that one on the first position then, you got it, redraw your hand and start again.

Once you make it through all the fingers, it's not *Game Over*. Nope, start over. It seems like everyone wants to be a better, stronger, more balanced person but they are pretty clueless as to how to make it happen. Well, now ya know.

Oh, check your clock. What time is it right now? Yeah, that's what I thought. It's time for you to stop staring at these pages like KoKo the chimp and get busy. Redraw your hand on another sheet of paper. You can do the trace thing like in kindergarten. It's okay, we won't laugh. *hee hee* No really, g'head. *Haw haw* You can even draw knuckles and color your nails if you want. Write your five areas on your fingers and start to work on the pinkie. Put your hand where you can see it. Make copies so you can stash it everywhere so that you will have reminders of what your goal is.

Pretty soon you'll be back to where you started, but you will be at a totally different level of living. And then . . . go again.

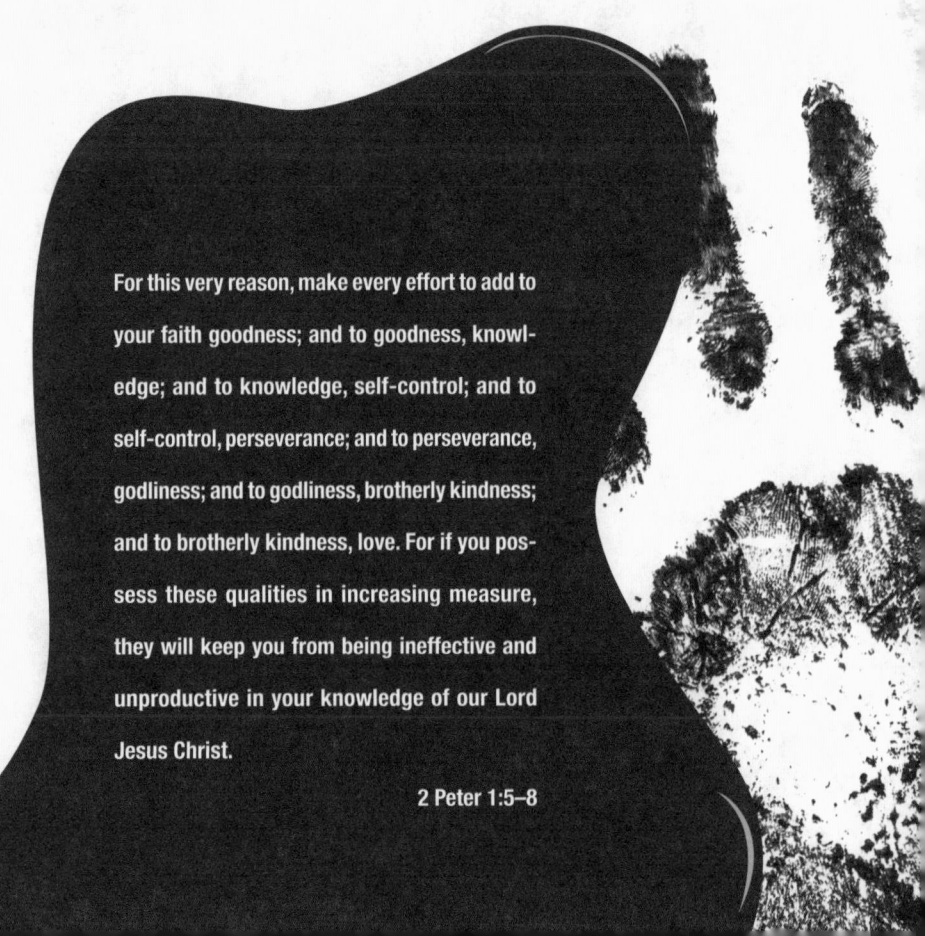

For this very reason, make every effort to add to your faith goodness; and to goodness, knowledge; and to knowledge, self-control; and to self-control, perseverance; and to perseverance, godliness; and to godliness, brotherly kindness; and to brotherly kindness, love. For if you possess these qualities in increasing measure, they will keep you from being ineffective and unproductive in your knowledge of our Lord Jesus Christ.

2 Peter 1:5–8

Reverse It!

This is opposite week. For an entire week, if you have a thought, do the exact opposite. C'mon, shake things up a little bit. Make sure it's nothing illegal, immoral, or totally stupid though.

But if someone is up there cranking out karaoke and you think, "I would never do that"—oh! Get up there and do it. If you hear about the party this weekend and you go out every weekend—oh! Sit at home with the fam. Whatever your normal routine is, do the opposite. It's like riding a roller coaster backward. It's a totally different view and a totally different rush.

You never know; it may even change your life. This is how I got into writing books. It's how my wife became a hardcore skydiver and my friend Glen started working at a church. I would never do that . . . 'oh!

Doorknobs Rule

I think the doorknob is the most underrated part of the whole house. In fact, if I could be any part of a building, I would want to be the door handle.

I bet there are a lot of knobs and handles that are pretty upset. They are sitting around waiting to see what part of a building or a home they will be, and the builder is like, "You . . . you're a doorknob." Can't you just imagine some of the reactions?

"Oh, c'mon, man! A doorknob? Dude, I have so much more to offer than just a doorknob. Just take another look. Give me a shot. How 'bout a hi-def TV? I could do that. Too much to ask? Okay, how about a table? Stick some legs on me and I'll make a killer table."

"Nope, you're a door handle."

Seems like a little bit of a downer. Oh, but no. Door handles control the world. Don't believe me? Then think of a world with zero door handles and zero knobs. You wake up tomorrow and they have all disappeared.

You get up to go to the bathroom and you can't get in. The door is shut and there's no knob. You go to the store and you push the door right open without a problem. But when you try to leave, problem—there's no handle. You have to wait for someone to come in and push it open so you can sneak out before it closes.

Door handles control the traffic flow of people. They control who comes in and who goes out. Oh, and put a lock on one . . . and it's got King Kong power. Yeah, to be a doorknob.

You know, you may be looking around at the gifts and abilities other people have and thinking, "C'mon, man, give me something to work with here." You think the stuff you are good at and the abilities you've been given aren't as cool or as important as someone else's. Hey, instead of looking at all the reasons that life sucks because you don't get to be like them, find all the reasons your talents are cool and how the world needs you to be good at what you are good at. Just remember, the world would screech to a halt if there were no more door handles and knobs.

The body is a unit, though it is made up of many parts; and though all its parts are many, they form one body. So it is with Christ. For we were all baptized by one Spirit into one body—whether Jews or Greeks, slave or free—and we were all given the one Spirit to drink. Now the body is not made up of one part but of many. If the foot should say, "Because I am not a hand, I do not belong to the body," it would not for that reason cease to be part of the body. And if the ear should say, "Because I am not an eye, I do not belong to the body," it would not for that reason cease to be part of the body. If the whole body were an eye, where would the sense of hearing be? If the whole body were an ear, where would the sense of smell be? But in fact God has arranged the parts in the body, every one of them, just as he wanted them to be. If they were all one part, where would the body be? As it is, there are many parts, but one body. The eye cannot say to the hand, "I don't need you!" And the head cannot say to the feet, "I don't need you!" On the contrary, those parts of the body that seem to be weaker are indispensable, and the parts that we think are less honorable we treat with special honor. And the parts that are unpresentable are treated with special modesty, while our presentable parts need no special treatment. But God has combined the members of the body and has given greater honor to the parts that lacked it, so that there should be no division in the body, but that its parts should have equal concern for each other. If one part suffers, every part suffers with it; if one part is honored, every part rejoices with it.

1 Corinthians 12:12–26

The Royal You

The Spirit himself testifies with our spirit that we are God's children. Now if we are children, then we are heirs—heirs of God and co-heirs with Christ, if indeed we share in his sufferings in order that we may also share in his glory.

Romans 8:16–17

Would you ever walk into a royal palace and insult the queen's kids right to their faces? Would you ever go up to the daughter of the king and put your hands up her shirt and unzip your pants and tell her that if she really liked you she would do it? Would you ever do something like that? Not if you wanted to keep breathing. Those guys standing around in suits who don't smile would love to hide your body somewhere. If you are in the presence of the royal family, you put on your best show. You don't do anything to offend them or degrade them.

You need to understand something and get it good. You are the adopted child of the King. That means you have full rights, royalty, and protection. You are important. You are valuable, pretty, strong, and worthy of the honor. This is a mega-moment that you really need to understand. Once you get it, you will be shocked by the way people treat you.

Listen, say you're at a party and somebody walks up to you with a red plastic cup and says, "Here, have a drink." Do you feel bad because you don't want the drink but you don't want to be rude? So you just sort of say, "No, thank you." And they start in with, "Oh, come on, just one, what's the big deal?" And you start feeling even worse. You don't want to hurt their feelings, and you have this internal conflict raging.

Get this in your head. You are royalty. You are the son or daughter of the most powerful King ever. You don't need to feel bad. How dare they give you something you didn't want! How dare they try to push you into something! You shouldn't feel bad. They should feel bad for being that stupid.

When you know who you are in God's family, it totally flips the script.

You've got this boyfriend or girlfriend you've gone out with a couple of times, and they want to take things further. You start kissing and making out, and your crush's hand starts moving really close to your . . . so you grab it and redirect it. After a few ticks the hand goes in for the kill again. This time you let it slide because you really do like the person and you really don't want them to feel embarrassed for getting called on it.

Hey, you are royalty! You have been adopted through the highest price—blood. You have nothing to feel bad about. Embarrassed? *They* should be embarrassed. How arrogant. How stupid for them to put you in that position. They should have their hand broken for even attempting such a thing. If they don't understand who you are and that they should be ashamed for doing that to you, then they gotta go! They are the ones who should feel bad, not you.

You are valuable. You are precious. You are royalty. And the only way others will know it is if you know it and believe it first. Then people had better recognize it and treat you that way, or they'll get their feelings hurt and look stupid.

CRASH TEST DUMMY

You've got a plan. Your parents are asleep, so one of your buds comes over and helps you push the car out of the driveway. You crank it up and you're off to your friend's house. You pick up your pals and you are rollin'. The music is blasting, everyone is hyped up and talking and laughing. You turn the corner and *SLAM!* Another car crashes right into your door and takes off.

You are totally not in a good place. The car is sitting in the middle of the road, and you guys are by yourselves. You slowly take out your cell and dial your parents' number. They've been asleep about three hours now. Oh, man, what are you gonna say?

Your dad answers the phone in his groggiest this-better-be-good voice and snaps out of bed when he hears your voice.

Your parents rush to the scene. They check to make sure everyone is okay. They get the car on the wrecker, and then you make that long, silent drive home.

You walk through the door and you break down. You tell them how sorry you are and how you know how much it hurt them and that you'll never do anything like that again. They hug you and tell you they forgive you and they don't think you are a horrible person.

Whew. Thank goodness that's over . . . or not. Yeah, they forgave you, but there is one major issue that is still unresolved. A jacked-up car. It is still wrecked and still needs to be fixed. To make that happen, you have to start working weekends and holidays to pay for the damage. You miss some parties, dates, and dances because of your mistake. It's not because you are being punished. It's just the natural consequences of what happened.

That's pretty much the way it is with sin. God will forgive you the very second you ask. But there are still consequences for your sin. Sometimes they are big and nasty, and other times they are barely noticeable.

If you go way too far and have sex, yeah, you may end up with some massive consequences. You may get a disease, get pregnant, or take a major reputation hit. Or the consequences may be more subtle. You may start closing off and not letting people get close to you. Maybe you slip into depression, but you never connect the dots that this stuff was a consequence of the sex. But like Ezekiel 44:12 says, "they must bear the consequences of their sin."

So if you ever blow it and bad things start happening, instead of getting all upset at God, look a little closer. It may just be the natural consequences of sin.

RETREAT . . . I MEAN, CHARGE!

A friend of my dad's received a National Medal of Honor for bravery in combat. He laughed as he told us what happened.

All the soldiers were stuck in foxholes. They were trying to get to the top of this hill, but they came upon a machine-gun nest and some snipers that were just picking them apart. The gunfight was going and they were hiding in holes, behind trees, anywhere they could find. He made it farther up the hill than the rest of the group. This meant he was taking a lot more heat. He was running low on ammo, so he decided that he was going to make a break for it and retreat back to where the others were.

He got psyched up, knowing that this would probably not end well. He counted to three, jumped out of his hole, and took off running. He took two steps and noticed that his entire company was now running up the hill. So he turned around and ran up the hill too. The enemy was so shocked that they had no time to react. It was surrender or die.

The U.S. military took the hill and secured a very strategic location.

After things calmed down a little, the men started coming over to him shouting, "You are the craziest man I have ever seen!" and "I thought we were gonna die out there until you charged the hill!"

Wait—"charged the hill"? Everyone thought that he had jumped up to lead the charge. They were so excited that they followed him into battle. To this day they still think he rushed the machine-gun nest. He never had the heart to tell them that he was hightailing it out of there and they misunderstood what he was doing.

Take a little scan of your friends. Do you have a lot who are Christians but really don't take a stand? They'll still go drink and party. They still get into the sex stuff with whoever they are crushing on at the moment. They still don't dig too deep or too often into the Word of God.

It may *not* be that they are just anti-committed. They may be waiting for someone to jump up and make a move. It may not take a huge move. Just take a stand for what is right, for what is God, and you'll be amazed at how many people will follow you.

David was just a teen who decided to take a stand. He went out with some rocks and a slingshot and knocked a giant on his back. And then watch what happened, "Then the men of Israel and Judah surged forward with a shout and pursued the Philistines to the entrance of Gath and to the gates of Ekron. Their dead were strewn along the Shaaraim road to Gath and Ekron" (1 Samuel 17:52). One kid stood up, and it gave these wimps the courage to be warriors. Take a stand.

#47 Directionally Challenged

I hate directions. I hate them! I hate them! They don't make sense to me. My brain doesn't function that way. I hate them.

Now, I love to drive. And when I don't have to be somewhere at a certain time, it's great, because I am sure I will take a couple of alternate roads. I'll turn around a few times and it's cool. Just part of the journey, and I get to see stuff I have never seen before.

Here's the weird part. In the exact moment that I make a wrong turn, I am confident that I am right. And as soon as I make the turn I'm like, "D'oh!" I get frustrated and feel stupid. And then when I turn around, I convince myself it's the other direction. In fact, driving here to write these pages, I knew where I was going. I was rehearsing it over and over, then right at the last minute I panicked—"Oh no, that's my exit!" I crossed three lanes of traffic to get off, only to go, "D'oh!" Wrong exit.

This drives me crazy. It's like the directions people give me don't connect until I've already messed up.

Don't get me wrong. My directional challenges go way beyond north, south, east, and west. There are so many days that I know the directions God gives me in his Word and I set off on my day focused on doing what is right. And then right at the last moment, I panic and do something else, only to go, "D'oh!" But in the moment I really think I am making the right decision. Oh, but no.

← N

I thought I was going loony until God explained it to me in Isaiah. In chapter 55, verses 8 and 9, he says, "For my thoughts are not your thoughts, neither are your ways my ways. . . . As the heavens are higher than the earth so are my ways higher than your ways and my thoughts than your thoughts."

So maybe I'm normal. That fight in me to take control and go, "No, this is what I need to do," is normal for us because God's ways are different from mine.

Well, here we go with some retraining the mind stuff. When there is something that you 100% "know" you are supposed to do or say but you've already had a direction from God, stick to what you heard first, not what you thought in the heat of the moment. See where it gets you. Because most of the time God doesn't give you a direction and then right at the last moment shout, "Turn here!" and change it. Go with what you know, and don't let your mind change God's direction. You will end up right in the middle of God's will.

HERO
TO ZERO

Win this game and we would go to the state basketball tournament. There were 7 seconds left on the clock. We were ahead by 3 points. And I was at the free throw line. All I had to do was make one free throw, and we would win the game. This is what little boys dream of. Time to be the hero.

The coach called a time-out. We were in the huddle and I told him I needed a drink. I took off and they made the plan. When I came back the coach gave me the quick story and I ran onto the court.

I could already feel the pride. I was the youngest guy on the team, and it was my moment. The ref gave me the ball. I bounced it a couple of times, and as I looked from the floor toward the rim, my eyes locked on the cheerleader that I had been crushing on for two years. All of a sudden my life turned into a cheesy teen sitcom. The noise of the gym faded into the background. She started to move in slow motion, jumping up and down, her hair flowing through the air as if it were in water. And all I could hear was her shouting, "Come on, Justin, you can do it!" I smiled and actually thought to myself, "Make this shot and I will get the girl."

I bounced the ball again, the noise in the gym came rushing back, and I took aim. I breathed in deeply and let the ball go, knowing the game was won and I was a hero. The ball arched toward the goal, right on target . . . and two inches short. It bounced off the front of the rim. A guy on the other team grabbed the ball and blew right past me. I turned and stood there as I watched him weave down the court . . . 4 . . . 3 . . . he spins around . . . 2 . . . 1 . . . he shoots . . . buzzer . . . SWOOSH! Tie game at the buzzer, and we lost the game in overtime.

> "Do you know that in a race all runners run, but only one gets the prize? Run in such a way as to get the prize. Everyone who competes in the games goes into strict training. They do it to get a crown that will not last; but we do it to get a crown that will last forever. Therefore I do not run like a man running aimlessly; I do not fight like a man beating the air. No, I beat my body and make it my slave so that after I have preached to others, I myself will not be disqualified for the prize."
>
> I Corinthians 9:24–27

I went from hero to zero in 7 seconds. I didn't think I could show my face at school ever again. But I did. I lived and I learned some valuable lessons about winning in everyday life.

Stick to Your Routine

I had never asked to get a drink of water during a game before. Even as I was going to get it, something didn't feel right. It was weird. So I was a little off-balance just from this little thing.

> "Very early in the morning, while it was still dark, Jesus got up, left the house and went off to a solitary place, where he prayed."
>
> Mark 1:35

When it comes to your relationship with Christ, stick to your routine. Figure out when you are going to pray, read the Word, and connect with God. Then do it at the same time every day. That will help you stay balanced when the stressful times hit.

Hang with Your Team

I left the huddle and was totally isolated from the team. If there was any moment I needed to know what was going on, it was that one. There were four guys on the court that were connected, and then there was me.

> "Let us not give up meeting together, as some are in the habit of doing, but let us encourage one another."
>
> Hebrews 10:25

Get a group of buds who are totally living for and following God. Not perfect, but trying to be perfect. Ones you can trust, who you can tell stuff to and it won't be a prob, who will always have your back. Then stick with them, especially when the pressure is on and your tendency will be to isolate yourself—that is exactly what the opponent, the Enemy, wants you to do.

Stay Focused on the Prize

I got distracted by the wrong prize. My focus was winning the cheer-leader, not winning the game.

> "Watch out that you do not lose what you have worked for, but that you may be rewarded fully."
>
> 2 John 1:8

Stay focused on reading the Word, praying, and living and growing closer to God. Hey, without that, you've got nothing. With that, "life to the fullest" is yours, and so is the prize.

Don't Be a Spectator

When things went wrong, I froze. I stood there and just watched what was going on. I was so blown away that the ball didn't go in that I became a spectator and watched the game go by.

> **"As the Philistine moved closer to attack him, David ran quickly toward the battle line to meet him. Reaching into his bag and taking out a stone, he slung it and struck the Philistine on the forehead. The stone sank into his forehead, and he fell facedown on the ground."**
>
> *1 Samuel 17:48-49*

When things go wrong around you and you feel the pressure of life, don't freak. Get moving. Keep playing the game and living your life. When something bad happens, don't just quit and decide being a Christian isn't worth it, it's too hard. Hey, the game is still on, and if you keep playing you will win!

Those were some tough lessons to learn. But I would much rather learn them on the court. I sill think about that game and how I would change so many things about those 7 seconds. But I quickly turn my thoughts from trying to change the past to how I can direct my future. What I learned from that game gives me the confidence to stay in the game and no matter what comes up, to keep following Christ.

> **"Forgetting what is behind and straining toward what is ahead, I press on toward the goal to win the prize for which God has called me heavenward in Christ Jesus."**
>
> *Philippians 3:13-14*

#45
You Have a Right to Know

Today ask these questions to at least ten people.
Don't crack a smile, and press them for an answer.

- If a turtle loses his shell, is he naked or homeless?

- If someone with multiple personalities threatens to commit suicide, is this considered a hostage situation?

- If you are cross-eyed and dyslexic, can you read normally?

- Why do we drive on a parkway and park on a driveway?

- Why do we call them apartments when they are all stuck together?

- For girls only: Why is it that when you put mascara on, your mouth opens?

- If vegetarians only eat vegetables, what do humanitarians eat?

Compile your answers and email them to your congressman with a note asking, "What do you plan on doing about this?"

Human Overhauling

Redesign Issue

If your knees bent the other way . . . what would a chair look like?

Get with some friends and redesign a chair. Meanwhile, if other major issues need to be adjusted, make the additional changes to the body as needed in order to complete the project.

Bonus

Think of all the other things that have to be redesigned because of the new knee configuration. Tackle and correct some of these issues.

Double Extra Bonus

If you know someone with a really cool shop, get them to help you make a prototype of your new chair.

Note: Redesigning anything that is already naturally made will be quite difficult and will take some intense concentration. This assignment will definitely prove that when God does something, he uses the best design possible. Good luck.

Big Toe Tantrum

Big Toe →

I broke my toe! It hurts. I'm stupid. And I broke my toe.

I need to come up with a good story. "I was in the belly of a killer wave when everything crashed around me, splintering my board and breaking my toe." Or how 'bout this? "There was a kitten stranded in the middle of the interstate. Death was certain if something wasn't done and done fast. So I jumped the fence, dodged the cars, grabbed the kitten, and dove into the grass, but as I was fully extended in my Superman dive, the mirror of a speeding car clipped my toe, breaking it as I rolled to safety with the precious kitten."

#43

Cute animal. Near death experience. Go with that one.

Yeah, I like those stories. They are so much cooler than the truth. And way less embarrassing.

Have you ever lost your cool? I'm not talking a little upset or mad. I am talking have you ever flipped out? Hopefully not, but probably so. I did and it wasn't good.

Emily and I were having a bad day. One thing piled on another, and I said things to and about this woman God gave to me as a gift that I wouldn't say about my worst enemy. She lashed back at me, and the gloves came off. I snapped, crackled, and popped all over her. And then, in my next show of Christian maturity, I stormed out of the room and headed upstairs, at which point I began a real show of manhood. I needed to take out my aggression on something. I was on the steps and thought, "Yeah, that's the ticket, the steps." So I reared back and kicked the stairs as hard as I could—SNAP! Oh yeah, I heard it. And in case I didn't, my toe went ahead and shot pain messages to my brain and told on me.

I hopped up the stairs, still holding the watch I had been trying to put on. I was so mad and flipped out that I threw it at the wall. A big wall. A large-surface-area wall. Not a hard place to miss . . . well, I did. Sitting on the desk right in front of the wall was my $2,500 high-speed, super-thin, pimped-out computer. I had the entire wall to shoot at, but the watch chose to target the 8- X 10-inch section where the computer was proudly displayed. Both the watch and the computer shattered.

Broken-toed, broken-watched, broken-computered, and broken-egoed, I sat looking at my $2,500 tantrum. And then I sat on a plane, heading to a conference where I was supposed to tell people how to live a Christian life and claim godly principles. But the questions and accusations kept coming.

"So what about the whole 'love is patient, love is kind' stuff?"

"What happened to 'love your wife as Christ loved the church,' huh?"

"Did I miss the part where it says, 'Love calls people names. Love accuses people and yells. It kicks the stairs, throws watches, breaks computers, and tries to hurt other people'?"

There's a reason that God gives us easy-to-understand definitions of love. It's a checklist. "Love is patient, love is kind. It does not envy, it does not boast, it is not proud. It is not rude, it is not self-seeking, it is not easily angered, it keeps no record of wrongs. Love does not delight in evil but rejoices with the truth. It always protects, always trusts, always hopes, always perseveres. Love never fails" (1 Corinthians 13:4–8). If what you're doing doesn't fit with the list, then it's not love. Saying you love them won't matter because your actions speak so much louder than your words.

Yes, I said I was sorry and I groveled and cried for forgiveness. And you know what? Emily doesn't even remember it. I guess *she* understands what the Scripture means when it says love keeps no record of wrongs.

#42
Will Your Crush Crush You?

Will your crush crush you? Odds are, *yes*. I know, there is a chance that this could be *the one*. So if you are going to set yourself up for success, you need to understand what the face of failure looks like. Get this in your head and you'll have a better shot at being the crush that can't be crushed.

The Eyes Have It

Hear Ye, Hear Ye

He Nose My Spirit

Yakkity-Yak

The FACE of Failure

Yakkity-Yak

Telling your crush everything about yourself may seem like a good idea at first. But this information overload could be the thing that separates you. When you go too deep too soon, some girls will have a tendency to go into a super-soul-connection mode that could really freak a guy out. Meanwhile, a guy usually snaps into chase-n-win mode, but with the overshare, it's game over.

Oh no, ... not super-soul-connection mode.

No joke man.

The experts tell us that the lovey-gushy feelings of a relationship last about two years. So let that be a gauge for how long it should take you to dish out the goods. Yeah, that seems like forever. But it's also easier than giving your crush all your secrets only to hear them in the locker room after you break up.

The Eyes Have It

The Bible says if your eye causes you to sin, poke it out. Well, what if the thing that causes you to sin is . . . uh . . . lower?

Sex creates a soul connection. That's the way God planned it. And the eyes are the window to the soul. It makes sense that Scripture starts with the eyes and then moves to the hands. Because that is how sex sin goes. That is how all sin pretty much flows. It starts with the eyes and moves to the hands way before it goes anywhere else.

> If your right eye causes you to sin, gouge it out and throw it away. It is better for you to lose one part of your body than for your whole body to be thrown into hell. And if your right hand causes you to sin, cut it off and throw it away. It is better for you to lose one part of your body than for your whole body to go into hell.
>
> Matthew 5:29–30

This soul connection that sex creates only works as an attraction when it is blessed by marriage. Otherwise it repels two people like magnets pushing each other apart. Protect your eyes and your soul. Save sex for the after-party—the one you'll have after you're married.

Hear Ye, Hear Ye

If you really want to set yourself up for a game of relational rugby, then make sure you only hear what you want to hear. Ignore the fact that your friends don't like your new affection. Think your parents are way overprotective and just don't want you to grow up. Forget that he is a total jerk to everyone. Or that she is catty and rude.

Don't be blinded by your rose-colored glasses. If everyone is singing the same song about your crush, maybe they are willing to see what you want to ignore.

He Nose My Spirit

One of the fastest ways to get imbalanced intimacy is to create a deep spiritual bond with your crush. Don't get me wrong; you want to be with someone who is strong in their faith, but you want it to be *their* faith. Totally separate from you. When you start spending a lot of time together praying ... alone ... in secluded, mood-filled locations ... you are dancing with disaster. Take your time and don't rush into praying with them. This could lead you to the *we-are-meant-to-be-together* syndrome because you connect in such a "real" way. You are creating a connection that should be reserved for your mate. Consider it your spiritual virginity and save it!

Keep this face in mind the next time you start building your perfect life with the next Mr. Right or you build a bond with the next Ms. Forever. It will help protect the core of who you are—who God made you to be—and it will help keep you from getting crushed by your crush.

The FACE of Failure

#41 DUCT TAPE

It's a cure-all. Just ask a dude. When life seems to fall apart, get the duct tape. Windshield is broken? Duct tape. Need a belt? Duct tape. Girlfriend talks too much? Uh . . . never mind. But ask any dude. If duct tape had been invented in 1912, the Titanic would not have gone down.

I really don't think the chicas fully understand the importance of duct tape to our society. But today you shall.

Here's your mission for today. Get a group of your friends—a group of guys and a group of girls. Give yourselves six minutes to come up with as many possible uses of duct tape as you can. Then, after you compare your answers, give each group a roll of duct tape and have them make their own creations. Go.

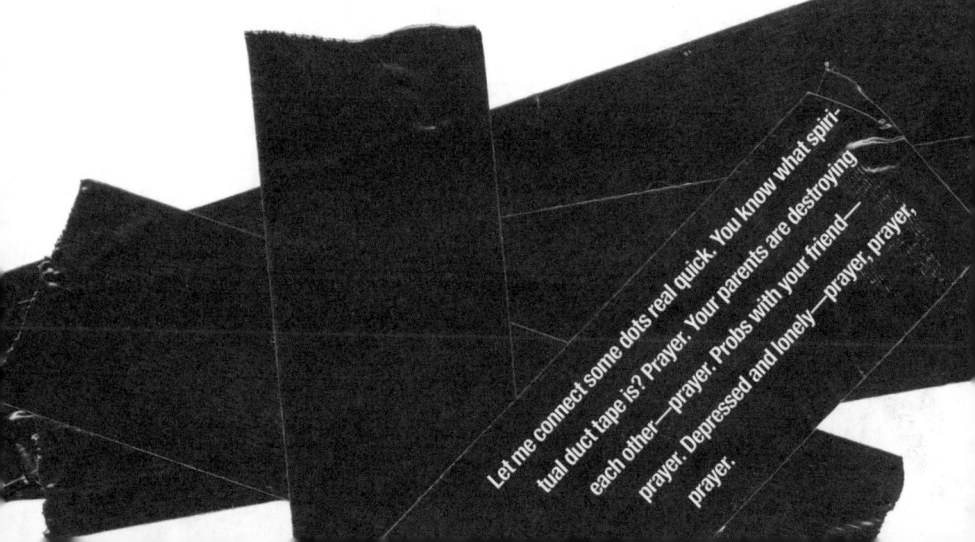

Let me connect some dots real quick. You know what spiritual duct tape is? Prayer. Your parents are destroying each other—prayer. Probs with your friend—prayer. Depressed and lonely—prayer, prayer, prayer.

Live It Full

Man, I love life. I love pushing it to the fullest. You hear everyone talking about living on the edge-forget that. Jump! Now that's what I'm talking about. Anything with a little risk involved, I'm in. Skydiving. Rock climbing. I love jumping off cliffs into rivers. I have a big four-wheel-drive Blazer to climb things and a motorcycle to cruise through the hills. I love this stuff. And man, when I was single, I loved going up and talking to that hottie for the first time, getting her number and asking her out. It scared the crapoodle out of me, but oh well, what a rush!

That's what life is all about. Feeling alive. But we, as the humanoids we are, we're pretty lazy. We'll take the easiest way possible to get what we want. I know I'm getting a little out there, but hang with me. The dots will connect.

When we start growing up, we go through all kinds of stuff. Crawling, walking, diapers, toilets, schools. And each new stage brings a lot of risks. When we hit the teen years, the world just opens up. There are so many things you can get into. Risks galore. Something inside of you just wants to be your own person and try new stuff. This is when people start getting into a lot of stupid stuff. Drugs, alcohol, tobacco, sex, the whole deal. They get this feeling . . . this feeling . . . Okay, when they start . . . oh, man, I am lost. I totally don't know where I was going with this. Those of you who have heard me speak know that this is pretty normal. I've just never done it while writing. Well, there's a first time for everything. So I guess I'm done. If you can come up with where I could have been going, hey, finish this and email me.

Okay. I gotta go now.

Oh, hey. I know what I was going to say. A lot of people think God threw all of these rules and regulations at us in the Bible and cut out all the fun. That is so not what happened.

See, God knew that there were things in this world that, if we did them, would attach strings to us. And each string would make us drag that sin around with us. And the more we sinned, the more strings and the more our life would be weighed down. So when he would say Don't do this or Don't do that, what he was saying was don't let this string get attached to you and slow you down.

The rules are there not to cut out the fun. They are there to cut out all the stuff that would hold you back. This gives you freedom. You are free to live life to the fullest without anything dragging you down.

#39 ER

Your parents are freaking out. They're running around yelling. Dad goes and starts the car. Mom grabs your little brother in her arms. You run ahead opening all the doors. Everyone jumps in the car as your dad puts the hammer down and you go flying to the hospital. Mom is holding your brother, Dad is driving like he's on a speedway test run, and you are sitting there quietly.

The car slides to a stop in front of the hospital. You dash through the doors into the ER. You are shuffled to a back room where the doctor has just arrived on a helicopter from across the country.

He looks at the boy and asks your parents what's wrong. They take a deep breath, look at each other with a hint of joy, and say, "Nothing. Absolutely nothing."

The doc looks at your parents and tells them to follow him. He walks them into the waiting room full of the sick and injured. He points and says, "I came here for them. They're the ones who need a doctor."

Matthew, the one in the Bible, was a tax collector. Back in the day, not only were they disliked for being the tax man but they were crooks. They would charge people way too much and then keep the profit.

Well, Matthew had a few of his buds over, and Jesus came with them. They were eating, laughing, and having a great time, and the Pharisees, the holier-than-thou-crew, saw it and were like, *"How can he sit there and even be associated with such sick and horrible people?"*

Jesus caught an ear of what was happening, and he hit them in front of everyone. "It is not the healthy who need a doctor, but the sick. I have not come to call the righteous, but sinners." Mark 2:17

Hey, who are you reaching out to that needs a doctor? Not like some kid with the bird flu but like what Jesus was talking about. The sinners. The sick. The people who are really hurting. They're the ones who need it the most. Not the healthy, secure, solid Christians.

Is it okay for your best buds to be solid believers? Yeah. In fact, that is the way it should be. But you're not reaching anyone if you go to your Christian school, attend your Christian church, hang with your Christian friends, listen to your Christian music, shop at your Christian stores, and never have any contact with someone who is not a follower of Christ.

If you want to follow Jesus that means you have to go where Jesus went. And that means reaching out to those who aren't perfect little Christians. It means going out and being with people who need him in a big way. Now get out there and take Jesus to some hurting people.

Dinner Delight

Tonight's dinner menu is very special. To start you off we have 1/2 cup of our finest lard. We will then move to our main course of 3 raw eggs and 2 squares of chocolate, chased down with 3/4 cup of sour milk and 2 tablespoons boiling water.

Oh, and for dessert we have 1 1/2 cups of sugar mixed with 1 teaspoon of baking soda, covered in 2 cups of flour and drizzled with 2 teaspoons of vanilla.

Yes! Your culinary dreams have come true! Sounds delish, right? Uh, not so much.

Well, take all those things, throw 'em in a bowl, stir it all up real nice and smooth, let it bake in the oven at 350 degrees for a few ticks, and watch out, mama! You'll end up with a cake so good it'll make you wanna slap your pappy.

How does it all work together like that? I dunno. All I know is it works in a pretty tasty way.

Check this out. Your life is a cake to God. He's got some sweet stuff going in it. Maybe some really cool stuff that has happened to you. Then there's some stuff that is yuck-o, kinda like taking a big ol' bite of straight flour. Maybe your parents have gone through a divorce. Then you chased it down with some raw eggs and sour milk, like getting into sex and partying. Then you got some life ingredients that smelled really good, like being popular, but it went bad with all the gossiping and backstabbing.

Yeah, if you pulled any single ingredient out of your life, it would look pretty messed up. But you are not just a grocery sack full of a bunch of ingredients. You are a cake. He will take all of the things in your life and mix them together, and with some time and, I am sorry to say, a little heat, all the ingredients you have experienced will work together, and you will end up with a pretty tasty life.

"And we know that in all things God works for the good of those who love him, who have been called according to his purpose."

Romans 8:28

Duck!
by Brooke

The first time I went golfing, I hit a duck. In the air. In mid-flight. Don't think that this bird was just sitting in the water and got startled as my golf ball skipped in the pond. No. This bird was in the air, flying, as my golf ball thunked off of its side. Do you realize the odds of that happening? Those are 1 in 154,389,000 odds!! (Okay, I made up those numbers, but it has to be something around that.)

For the rest of my game, I kept thinking about that duck. How it made that thunking noise, the quack that was a mixture of surprise and pain, the splash of the water as the duck came in for a crash landing. Anytime that I lost focus and started reliving the drive-by duck-ing (get it? Drive . . . driver . . . golf . . . oh, forget it!), I would start to hit the ball off the course. It would go in the bushes, off a tree, bouncing down the sidewalk . . . it was pathetic.

The truth of the matter is, there was nothing that I, Brooke, could have done about that duck. I had no possible way of knowing it was going to be flying at the exact moment I hit off the tee. It was truly an honest mistake. I could drive myself crazy thinking that if I had just waited a second, or had taken less practice swings, I never would have clocked that bird. All of

Fore

that thinking didn't do me any good; all it did was ruin the rest of my game.

Ducks are going to fly in front of your shot from time to time. It's a part of the game, but you have to realize that your whole game can and will suffer if you spend the whole time thinking about the one incredibly crazy shot that you couldn't possibly have predicted. There were more holes on the course than just that one with the pond. But because I couldn't get past it, my whole game was ruined. When you have eighteen holes to play, you can't lose focus on one bad shot.

Your life will have more surprises than all the golf games you could ever play. So if you take a bad shot or make a bad choice, don't spend your life reliving the manic moment. Put it behind you, let it go, and keep moving on to the next shot.

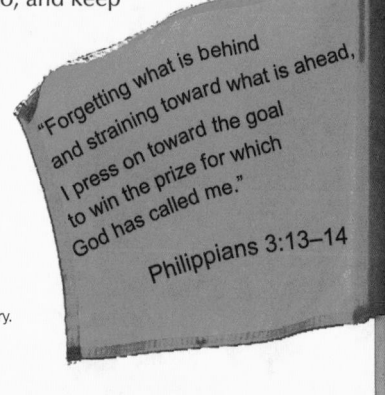

"Forgetting what is behind and straining toward what is ahead, I press on toward the goal to win the prize for which God has called me."

Philippians 3:13–14

PETA Note: The duck was not hurt in the writing of this story. It flew off after it hit the water. I promise!

"I thank God every time I remember you."
Philippians 1:3

Emily

Thank you for being my love, my life, my rock, and my feather pillow. You didn't know what you were getting into when you hooked up with me, but God did. When he made you my "crazy waitress," he was working his plan. Thank you for being my cheerleader and for the excitement that fills up this life we call a ministry. I hope I can bring you just a fraction of the happiness you've brought to me. Frogs in snow boots! You're my best friend.

Mom and Dad

Yet again, thank you for raising me to know that there is nothing I can do, but with Christ anything is possible. You are the reason I am the way I am. Yep, I blame you. Thank you for growing more and more as my spiritual guides and for continuing to grow yourselves, if not for me, for those two little boys, Tate and Trent, that I call nephews and you call grandsons.

Allan

You rock! Thank you for being my agent. I know I am not the easiest person to work with—heck, even to get ahold of. But more than that, thank you for being a mentor, a friend, someone to yell at and laugh with. You have taught me the art of asking, "What's in it for you? How can I help you?" I will never be able to repay you and Shauna for what you have done for us. We love you.

Brooke

Thank you for being insanely sane. You have an unbelievable talent in writing and connecting with people. Since the first time you fell off my stage you left an impact on me . . . well, I guess it left an impact on you too, but anyway, thank you for giving so much to me and to others. Go big. Try something skygantic. Who knows, it might just work.

Ed Young Jr.

Thanks for walking in the light you've been given and dreaming big in creating a place like Fellowship Church. It's a place that I get revived, re-amped, and refueled. Thank you for showing me the importance of "team" by surrounding yourself with guys like Preston, Pace, and the whole student ministry crew and giving them the freedom to do what God has made them good at. Rock on!

Mark Hall

Thanks for taking the time out of your two-week whirl-wind Casting Crowns tour to drop in and give me some words. You always amaze me and inspire me to do more. And when we talk, you make me feel normal, because no topic has to be discussed for more than 32 seconds. Hey, your ADD is surpassed only by your songwriting skills. I am still waiting for the song that incorporates "Lookadoo" in it. Future Grammy, right there. Much love.

Rob and Gayle, Tommy and Christa, Paul and Wez, Tom and Elizabeth

Thank you for giving of what you have: homes, time, food, and Jeeps. You guys poured so much into my life in a very short time. Thank you for letting me get away and hide and get some words down on paper. You will never know what a difference you made.

Jesus

Thank you for giving your life for me. Even when I spit in your face, you still forgive me. (See #30.) Thank you for never leaving me and that what I see as horrible stuff, you use to make your plans work out. (See #38.) Thank you for letting me be a part of your plan.

Now it's your turn. Who do you need to give ups to? And if you think, *Oh, they know*, then that is the perfect person to send a note to. Knowing it and hearing it are totally different. Tell them thank you, and be specific in the "for what" section.

So who do you have? Teachers? Parents? Friends? Baggers at the grocery store?

Get a pen, pencil, markers, any writing utensil of your choice and put it on paper. Send it to them and let them know they are a big deal to you.

Make it last! Send them a card or note. Something they can hang on to or stick on the wall. Voice messages, texts, IMs, and emails just kinda get lost in the shuffle. Give 'em something they can go back to over and over.

"In all my prayers for all of you, I always pray with joy because of your partnership in the gospel from the first day until now, being confident of this, that he who began a good work in you will carry it on to completion until the day of Christ Jesus." Philippians 1:4–6

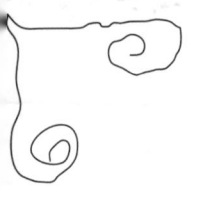

35

Crazy for Cotton

Let's take something random, like . . . cotton. (I just saw a cotton commercial on TV, so cotton it is.) Let's get this fluffy stuff and process it, and let's add some, let's see, let's add some linen. We'll get it all softened up and gooey, and then let's roll it out with a rolling pin until it is totally flat. Flat as a pancake . . . no, flatter. Like a sheet of paper. So flat you can almost see through it.

Grab some markers and start drawing on it. Put some little squiggly lines, and put some numbers on it. Write on it. Oh, and draw a picture of someone famous. It can be someone old, like Arnold Schwarzenegger. Or go with someone young, or even throw Mickey on it. Hey, do this. Take your sheet and cut it into four or five rectangles and make each one of them different.

Now get your pictures and walk outside. And as you walk outside, imagine thousands of people rushing you, trying to get your little pieces of paper. They start fighting and killing people just to get your paper.

And when someone gets your paper, lots of people will do anything that person says. It's like it holds some magical power. Some people won't do anything the paper holder says. In fact, they start shouting about how evil your paper is. Other people start plotting and scheming about how to get the other people's paper.

Wow, all that over some cotton and linen paper that you drew all over. Sounds pretty freaky . . . or does it?

Change Arnold's face into Benjamin Franklin's, change your random number into a serial number, and throw "100" in the corners, and you have the same chaos. The same level of love, hate, and deception, all

_Baa

over little pieces of paper made of 75% cotton and 25% linen.

What makes the difference? Oh, yeah, it's money. So? It's still just pieces of paper with pictures. What gives it any value?

Snap to the next random thought. Can you imagine what life was like before money?

How much is that cow worth?

It's worth three hogs.

How much is a hog worth?

Eight chickens.

How much is a chicken worth?

Three buckets of grain.

Okay, so that means if I want to buy a cow, I need to get 72 buckets of grain. Or I could go with 24 buckets, 1 hog, and 8 chickens.

Finally someone said, Okay, this ain't working. We need to have one system. One currency that everything is valued at. And to make the paper worth it, we will back it up with the valuable goods. And the strength of the wealth of the governing board will let us know that the paper has value.

That's not the best lesson in economics, but it's pretty close to the story of Jesus, in a messed-up Lookadoo way.

In the Old Testament, sin was kind of like a trading system, but not really. See, sin meant death. When sin happened, it had to be paid for, so something had to die. That's why they would take the most perfect of the perfect animals and sacrifice them, and the animals would pay the bill for us. And it became pretty chaotic.

Okay, how much is this sin worth?

Two perfect lambs.

How much is a perfect lamb worth?

Twelve perfect doves.

Well, what's a perfect dove worth?

And the system didn't seem to be working.

So God, being the smart God he is, said it was time for a new system. He said, "There is going to be one currency. One blood. I am going to send my Son, Jesus. He's going to live and go through everything you do as a human. He is going to remain pure and perfect; then the people I send him to will kill him. That will be the one sacrifice, the one death, the one blood. And then to show you that I have the value covered and that no one else can counterfeit the currency, I am going to raise him from the dead. I will let him walk around on Earth, be seen, do a couple more cool things, and then I am going to snatch him up.

"Now all you have to do is put your trust in this currency, this one shot, blood-covering-all-sin currency, and you will be rich . . . high roller rich. In fact, your inheritance will be a little slice of heaven—no, literally a piece of heaven."

I guess I wonder why we go so crazy over paper and ink, yet we are pretty mellow about a one-time currency change that is backed up by the God who pulled off the biggest mind-blower of all: Jesus . . . cross . . . blood . . . dead . . . raised . . . done!

Okay, I know god may not have said it exactly like that but I bet it was something close.

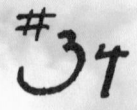

THE GIFTS OF THE WIZARD

A wizard sweeps you up into the clouds and tells you that he will give you anything you ask for. In fact, he has three stadium-sized caves in the mountains, and he tells you that he has already filled them for you. He wants to blow your mind, and everything's prepared. All you have to do is ask. Ask and he will give you anything in the caves.

Wow! You are totally excited, so you look at this powerful being and you say, "Okay, Mr. Wizard," and then you shout with excitement, "I want a new car!"

The wizard looks at you kind of strange and says, "A new car? I have the powers of the universe at my disposal, and you ask for a new car? I don't even have to look. There's not a new car in any of your caves. Try again. Ask for anything that I have stored for you and it's yours."

You think again. "Okay, then how about a perfect boyfriend?" (or girlfriend).

The wizard just blows past that one. "I don't have that for you. Come on. Ask for anything I have for you and it's yours."

You start to get pretty irritated at the wizard. He is saying that he wants to give you more than you could ever dream or imagine, but he keeps shooting down your requests. Do you give up? Do you tell him that he's just toying with you and he needs to drop you back into your old existence and leave you alone? Do you believe the wizard and keep trying?

You decide to try it again. The wizard says he wants to give you everything and he has huge stockpiles of blessings—all you have to do is ask. Finally, you have an idea. You walk up to the wizard and ask, "Can I see what's in the caves? I want what you have to give, but I am not sure what to ask for, so it would be a lot of help if I knew what you had."

"Of course," he laughs. "Come on, I'll show you everything." He

peels back the tops of the mountains one by one, and you almost pass out. There is so much that your eyes can't even process it all. You do notice a few things. You see a cure for your grandmother's cancer. You see a healthy little baby. You see a job where you are helping change people's lives and making money doing it. You see your five closest friends, and they all have "Christian" stamped on them. And the rest of the stuff is just too overwhelming. You turn away and fall on the ground exhausted.

The wizard tells you, "I'm going to leave my Spirit here to guard your treasure. Just come and ask for it in my name, and the Spirit will give it to you."

"This is the confidence we have in approaching God: that if we ask anything according to his will, he hears us. And if we know that He hears us—whatever we ask—we know that we have what we asked of him" (1 John 5:4–15).

"...ur own pleasures." James 4:2–3

"And I will do whatever you ask in my name, so that the Son may bring glory to the Father. You may ask me for anything in my name, and I will do it." John 14:13–14

and the door will be opened to you."

Luke 11:9

"So I say to you: Ask and it will be given to you; seek and you will find; knock

Are you connecting the dots? You gotta ask for stuff that will bring glory to God. And if you don't know what to ask for, ask God to show you what to ask for, and then ask for that. Do you get it? Ask!

"You do not have, because you do not ask God. When you ask, you do not receive, because you ask with wrong motives, that you may spend what you get on yo...

IS IT HOLY?

I get to hang out with a lot of groups in a lot of churches. Whenever I ask if they know kids who are into drugs, alcohol, sex, oral sex, cutting, and stuff like that, just about everyone says they do. And when I ask if they know Christian kids who are into that stuff, about the same number say yes. In fact, I even asked a group where they get the most pressure to compromise, from Christians or non-Christians. The answer: "Christians."

They said the non-Christian kids are cool with whatever. If you take a stand for something, they are pretty cool about it. The Christian kids, they said, will hound you, will make fun of you, and just won't let it go.

If you are reading this and you are the fake—you are the one into the partying, the sex, the gossiping—I have a question for you. "Is it holy?" See, I am so tired of Christians being fake. I am tired of girls saying they love Christ and then getting in their boyfriend's pants. I am tired of guys out chugging and puking, partying and going nuts, and saying that they are solid with Christ.

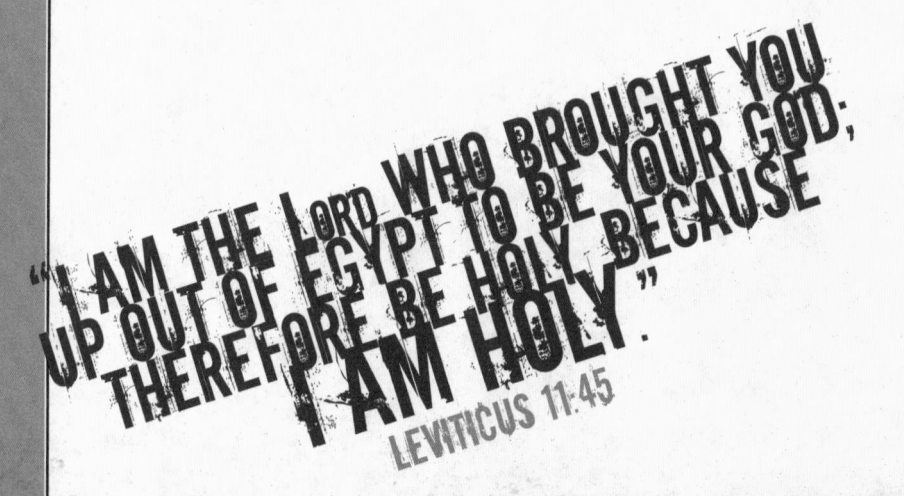

"I AM THE Lord WHO BROUGHT YOU UP OUT OF EGYPT TO BE YOUR GOD; THEREFORE BE HOLY BECAUSE I AM HOLY."
LEVITICUS 11:45

Listen, the Son of God was not massacred so you can pick and choose when to be Christlike and when it's okay to slip. God is after obedience. Total obedience.

Here, let's see if you've got what it takes to be obedient. With every sitch ask yourself, "Is it holy?"

Your friends are having a party. Their parents are out of town, and it's an "anything goes" party. Your crush will definitely be there. Do you go? I mean, c'mon, you're not going to be getting into all that crazy stuff, so it's okay, right?

Is it holy?

You're late. You sneak in the house totally after curfew. Luckily your parents are already asleep. The next day they ask you when you got home. Do you fudge the numbers just a little? After all, no one knows and it's not that big of a deal.

Is it holy?

Your buds are going to the movies. It's gotten rave reviews and it's PG, so everything is cool. In the flick a couple of people fall for each other and end up having sex . . . oh, I mean, making love. Do you go?

Is it holy?

I know, you think I'm way overreacting and getting too outta touch. After all, there's nothing wrong with going to a movie like that. Hey, the question is not if it's right or wrong. The question is, "Is it holy?"

Chillin' at the party, who cares if it's right or wrong—is it holy? Covering your lateness, not a big deal, but is it holy?

If you get to something in your life, one of those decision times, and you are like, *Well, it's not unholy . . .* that's not enough. God is looking for people who are totally committed. People who are willing to be holy as he is holy. Is it holy?

WELL?! Is it?

. . . Too Good . . . . . .

Pride. Arrogance. Ever met anyone who was totally conceited? They were all into themselves. They were great. Just ask them.

The ancient Proverb says, "Pride goes before destruction, a haughty spirit before a fall."

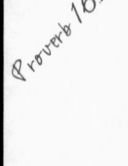

Proverb 16:18

Catch the visual of what that means.

I was going through airport security with my skydiving rig. I had it packed in a bag—for some reason people get nervous when you hop on a plane with a parachute strapped to your back, so I packed it up.

Now, the way the reserve parachute is rigged up, it looks like a bomb in the X-ray machine. There's always a big fuss. It has to be X-rayed several times. And then they will pull it out of the bag to make sure it is really a parachute. I knew it was coming, so I was ready for it.

As I went through the metal detector, I told the lady standing there that the bag the man was about to look at was a parachute. She told me to go tell the guy. So I got his attention and told him about the rig. And in the rudest, most arrogant, jerk-face way he snapped, "I know how to do my job. I don't need you to tell me how to do it."

I said, "Hey, she told me to let you know, that's all." I stepped back and waited.

He got to the parachute and he didn't even pause. He just let the conveyor belt keep rolling. He didn't check it. He didn't make sure the bomb-looking thing on the X-ray wasn't one. He just kept going. It was the easiest airport entrance I've had. I could have been carrying a bomb and he wouldn't have stopped me.

Don't miss what happened here. This dude had just popped off that he knew how to do his job and he didn't need any help. If he stopped to call someone over to check what he saw, then he would look like an idiot. See, your pride is the only thing that can make you look like an idiot.

Ya know, I wasn't the enemy on this flight. I was just some dude with a parachute. But at some point this guy's pride will be the thing that allows destruction. It will allow something to slip by because he was too arrogant to admit that he needed help.

It's okay to be confident. Confidence is cool. But when you start getting cocky, watch out. You are setting up a Humpty Dumpty kind of fall. And don't be afraid to ask for help. It's not a slam on you to admit that you don't know everything or that you can't blow through this life alone. Connect with others. Let them help you and you be willing to give them a boost.

For when I am weak, then I am strong.
2 Corinthians 12:10

#31

Cell Phone Celeb

Do you want to get people to notice you? To see you? To gawk at you like you are from another planet? Then you too are ready to become a cell phone celeb. Follow these simple steps and you will have people thinking you are a rude, pretentious snob in no time.

Always answer the phone. It doesn't matter where you are—the mall, an elevator, class, a funeral—always answer it. You want to subject all the innocent bystanders to your conversation, even if they don't care about who broke up with whom or what belly jewels you're getting.

Set your ringer loud. Set it on the loudest possible ring, and while you're at it, download some obnoxious song and let it blast as your ringtone. Then let it ring a couple of times so you get to hear your favorite hit. Don't worry if those around you don't have the same taste in music. Let it ring.

Cell yell! Talk on the phone as if you are still using a string and two cans (old school, baby!). It really makes people think you are cool when they have to listen because they don't have a choice.

Why do people yell into the phone when *they* are in a noisy place? Isn't it the person on the other end that should be yelling?

Never turn it off. Yeah, this will let people know that you are way too important and that you might receive that all-important phone call at any moment.

Always flash your phone. Make sure you use your phone as a status symbol. This will confirm to everyone how shallow and materialistic you are and that your only value is in the things you sport.

That should pretty much do it. If you wish to be annoying and irritating, that should help. And if you are having trouble getting the courage to follow these steps, then you need a good dose of pride. You need to understand that you have the right to do whatever you want, and if someone else thinks it's rude or it imposes on them, that's their problem. And make sure to always ignore Philippians 2:3: "Do nothing out of selfish ambition or vain conceit, but in humility consider others better than yourselves."

SPITTING ON THE CROSS

Would you ever spit on a cross? Really, think about it. You go into a church or someplace like that and there is a big cross standing there—would you walk up with a big ol' wad in your mouth and let it fly all over the cross? Visualize it. Shut your eyes and try to see yourself doing it. C'mon. God is not going to strike you dead, and there really is a point to it. Picture it.

Hey, don't keep reading until you get a visual. Try it.

Moving on.

Forget about the cross. What about Jesus? If you saw him walking by, would you launch a spit missile at him, watching it splat all across his face?

How 'bout this. Put Jesus on the cross. He is being tortured, abused, and killed for your sins. In the middle of this action, would you walk up and let one loose on him and start shouting, "That's not enough! Your sacrifice, your pain, it's worthless. You shouldn't have done it!"

Change channels really quick. Do you have something in your life, some sin, that you know is wrong and you choose to do it anyway? Got anything like that? I'm not talking about times when you slip or mess up and you are into something before you know it. I'm talking about things that you know are wrong and you do anyway. And there is that moment when your mind and spirit is like, *You need to stop. Don't do it . . .* and you do it anyway. Anything like that?

Sometimes it's even something you have to plan out in advance. Something like:

scheming on how to get back at that girl who started a rumor about you

planning a little sexy getaway with your bf/gf

looking for the next party to go get trashed at on the weekend

Well, guess what? If you know it's wrong and that God sure wouldn't give his thumbs up on it and you choose to do it anyway, then that is like you walking up to a bloody, beat-down Jesus, spitting right in his face, and saying, "You shouldn't have died like this. You wasted your time! It's not enough!"

Read that again. Get it in your mentals. Whenever you are about to do something and you feel that thing inside of you telling you it's not what God wants and you do it anyway, you need to see the visual of you walking up to the cross and spitting on your Savior.

Amp it up. If you really want to make a change and do something different, and if you have an issue that you have dealt with over and over and over, then do this. Get a cross. One that can be with you whenever this choice, this sin could happen. And if you walk up to that line and just blow right past it and sin anyway, then take your cross and spit on it. Don't just think about it. Do it.

For me it was the cross I wear around my neck. I had a revolving sin that I had been telling myself I would stop doing for years. I walked up to the line, ignored the Holy Spirit, and kept going. Immediately I took the cross off and forced myself to spit on it. I missed the first time so I made myself do it again. This was one of the hardest things I have ever done in my life. In fact, it made me sick. I mean, physically ill. But guess what, the very next time my favorite sin popped up, I didn't want anything to do with it. Thank you God!

Yeah, this may take a few tries, but you will eventually get tired of it and you will make a change.

What Would You Do?

You're walking down the street with your fam, minding your own business, when a group of skinhead Satan-worshipers surrounds you. They put a shotgun in your face, and they tell you that they are going to kill you and your family in a satanic sacrifice. But they tell you they will let everyone go if you do one thing. All you have to do is get down on your knees and pray to the evil one. You have to worship him, say that you offer your life to him, and reject Christ.

Do you do it? Remember, they have a shotgun ready to shoot your mom in the face. Do you do it? I mean, you could fake it, right? You can say the words and not mean it . . . or can you?

In the book of Daniel something like this really happened. These three buds were totally solid with God. The president of the day made a law that said when you heard certain music play, you had to drop down and worship the gold statue the prez had made. This meant *everyone*. And if you didn't do it, you'd be burned alive.

Well, the music played, the people fell, and there were three dudes still standing. The three buds, Shadrach, Meshach, and Abednego. They wouldn't do it. Can't you see their friends and family? *C'mon, kneel down! You don't really have to worship the idol, just get down here. Heck, just pray to God while you're down here. They'll never know.*

But they wouldn't kneel. They refused. They wouldn't compromise and try to blend in while keeping it holy. They stood up, knowing the consequences.

The president, King Nebuchadnezzar, found out, grabbed the three guys, and brought them in for questioning. He explained the law to them in detail. Then he described the consequences in even more detail. He reminded them how easy it would be to fall down and what a horrible death it is to be charcoaled alive.

And their response? "O Nebuchadnezzar, we do not need to defend ourselves before you in this matter. If we are thrown into the blazing furnace, the God we serve is able to save us from it, and he will rescue us from your hand, O king. But even if he does not, we want you to know, O king, that we will not serve your gods or worship the image of gold you have set up."

Daniel 3:16-18

Click! Nebi pulled the trigger. He took his shot and threw the guys into the pit.

Could you do that? Not in some Bible story kinda way. I'm talking about for real. Rewind . . . and . . . play. A psycho has a shotgun ready to blow you and your family away. All you have to do is bow down and worship something that is not God. Do you compromise? Do you bow down and just not mean it?

Something very important that you need to understand: You are invincible until God is finished with you. Let me repeat that in some big letters.

You are invincible until God is finished with you.

Nothing can touch you and no one can harm you.

The three friends knew that when they went to their own BBQ. Daniel knew it when he got tossed in with the lions. Gilligan knew it when he got put on the island . . . uh . . . scratch that last one. But know that nothing and no one can take you off this Earth if God says no.

If you really and truly grasp this, if you really understand it, man, your boldness and confidence will go nuclear. That's why when I was thinking about skydiving, I thought, *Why not? I am invincible till God is done with me.*

*Note to the senseless: Don't be stupid! If you do something like jump out of a plane without a parachute because you are invincible until God is finished with you, yeah, he could save you. He's God. But he would probably think, *If he's that stupid, why bother?* But in the normal stuff of life you can't be beat.

Back to the previous thought; don't turn back a page.

Now go back. You have a gun in your face. What do you do? Is a gun more difficult to deal with than a firey furnace? Is it trickier than a den full of ticked-off, starving lions?

No compromise. No shame. Just confidence and boldness that no matter what, God can save you. But what if he doesn't? Will you still say like Shad, Mesh, and Abed did in Daniel 3:18, "But even if he does not, we want you to know, O king, that we will not serve your gods or worship the image of gold you have set up"? What will you do when you feel like compromising to save yourself from pain, hurt, or the embarrassment of being thought of as weird? What will you do?

NO COMPROMISE
BOLDNESS

#28

Quitter

by Brooke

Hi, my name is Brooke and I'm a quitter.

You heard me right. I am boasting about being a quitter. If you had asked me a few years ago if I would ever brag about being a quitter, I would have looked at you like you were insulting me. But there are times in life when quitting is the strongest move you can make.

Volleyball had been my life for years. I dreamt about it, thought about it in school, talked about it to anyone who would listen. I played it, I coached it, I lived it. In practices I would give everything that I had every second of every practice. The harder I worked, the better I would become; the better I was, the stronger my team was. All through school I had been a captain of the team, looked to as a leader and as one of the better, smarter players. In practices when we could pick teams, I was the setter that everyone wanted on their team. I know you're probably thinking that I'm just bragging here, but if I don't tell you, how will you know? Every team I was on was a successful team that would go deep into the playoffs. And I loved my team. They were my sisters on the court. I would never let them get upset with a mistake, never let them think they couldn't do what they had to do. I was a motivator. So when I got to the point where my motivation was ripped away from me, I had to make a decision.

I got to the point where the person I was supposed to respect most in the game that I loved more than anything, the coach, was the person who was changing who I was in a negative way. No matter how hard I tried and no matter how much I gave in practice, I was made to feel like I was a failure. I gave it my all for as long as I could before I decided that it didn't matter anymore. I tried to talk to my coach in her office. I went to see what I could do to improve and to impress her. I was willing to do whatever it took. But when she threw a pen at me and started yelling, something inside of me changed. I figured that if I was going to get yelled at and spit on for doing my best, why waste the effort? I started jogging instead of sprinting. I started getting to practices late. I became the player that I had prided myself on not being. I became the player that I used to do my best to motivate. But I couldn't motivate myself anymore. I started snapping at my friends and being more negative. I was a different person. The sport I had once had such a passion for was now the worst part of my day. Just like it says in Psalm 17:22, "A cheerful heart is good medicine, but a crushed spirit dries up the bones." And my spirit was getting crushed.

One day after I had been thinking all day of a way to skip practice, I snapped to my senses. What was I doing? Who was I becoming? I didn't know, but what I did know was that I hated what was happening to me. I was letting myself be controlled by a negative situation. It was time for me to make the biggest decision of my life up to that point. Was I going to keep myself in this situation that was changing me for the worse, or was I going to do something about it?

After all of my options were tapped out, I knew what I had to do to regain my sanity. I had to be a quitter. I had to walk into my coach's office and tell her what was going on and that I could no longer subject myself to what was happening. It was the most difficult thing in the world to say "I quit" to my favorite sport, to say that my love for volleyball was being killed. But when I spoke to my coach and I watched her roll her eyes at me, I knew I was doing the right thing. It was like God was giving me my final sign that I was making the right call.

Some might think that the strong thing to do would have been to stay and finish out the season while being mentally and emotionally beaten down. But I knew that for me, the strong choice was getting myself out of that situation. I had the girls on the team tell me that they respected what I did and that they wished they had the guts to do the same. After I quit, four more girls on the team did the same. They had had enough too.

At times in life strength comes in making the right choice, not the easy one. Quitting was not easy, and it hasn't been since that day. But through all of this I realized that no good can come from voluntarily putting or keeping yourself in a negative situation. You have to be smart enough and strong enough to know when enough is enough.

WAR

You're surrounded. It's dark. All you see are tracer rounds, and you hear the chaos and explosions. You're holding your position. You have to trust that all your fellow warriors are doing the same. You are giving the enemy everything you've got. You are totally spent, but winning. Then, out of nowhere, you start catching fire from behind you. You're taking hits from both directions.

> "For our struggle is not against flesh and blood, but against the rulers, against the authorities, against the powers of this dark world and against the spiritual forces of evil in the heavenly realms."
>
> Ephesians 6:12

What happened? Somebody blew it. Somebody let the enemy get through. Now you are in the biggest fight of your life.

Fellas, we are in a major battle together. Check it: Porn, lust, masturbation, we think this is our own little battle that we are fighting in our own little corner of existence. Oh, but no. Anytime you are hit with a lust bomb, you are not alone. Thousands of Christian guys are getting hammered just like you at that very moment. It's an attack. And remember, this battle is a spiritual one, fought in the war zone we cannot see.

All of the other guys out there are getting pounded with porn, massacred with masturbation, or slaughtered with sex. They are fighting the same battle you are. And they are counting on you to hold off the enemy, because if you crack, you let the enemy behind our battle lines. And all of a sudden we are having to fight a battle on two fronts because you blew it.

You are not alone in this. And as a guy this is one of the biggest battles you will ever fight and, I'm sorry to say, the longest battle. It does get easier but it will never fully go away. We have to stick together on this one. We have to stand strong.

I'll do everything in my power to win the battles from over here. Don't let me and everyone else down by blowing it on your side. When we all fight together we get stronger. The only way to fully crush the enemy is for each one of us to win our fight. It's a single battle fought for every guy who is a soldier for Christ.

Battle Plan

I met a group of gutsy warriors in Virginia. They meet together every week, and as soon as they walk in they have to give a number: 235. 17. 3. 79. That is how many days they have won the battle. They totally hold each other accountable for winning their battle.

Another group in Texas has amped it up. They have started telling the numbers, and if someone has blown it, then they have to get in the middle and then . . .

1. Each guy in the group tells the dude exactly what they think about what he did and how he is blowing it and making their battle even harder.
2. They get a plan together to help the brother out.

Just thought you'd like to know what some others are doing.

Guys, if you are getting a group together let us know. Go to www .lookadoo.com and find the section "War Zone." Tell us what you are doing and give us all some words to bring power to the fight.

I Hate Stairs
Another little ditty by Brooke

26

I was watching daytime television the other day (hey, don't make fun!) and a talk show had the topic of phobias. They had guests on who were scared of weird things. This one girl was honestly terrified of ovens. Ovens! You know, those big boxes in your kitchen that produce homemade cookies! I can see how burning yourself might be a concern, but this woman was deathly afraid that the oven would come to life and eat her. I know, I laughed too! It made me wonder what kind of crazy childhood she'd had. It also made me think about what weird phobias I have. Let's see. What are some things that I'm scared about? I'm not scared of spiders; I think they're cool. The dark doesn't really get me. Heights? Yeah, extreme heights freak me out a bit, but that's not weird.

What's something weird that freaks me out? Hmmm. Well, there's stairs. I get nervous around stairs because in high school my friend used to think it was hilarious to try to trip me when I was going up the stairs. So every time I'm on some stairs, I have to hold on to the railing and look down at the stairs. I even get nervous if someone is behind me; I usually let them go so I can be in the back. I always imagine myself tripping and not being able to get any footing, then just face-planting into the corner of a stair over and over and over again as I helplessly somersault down the entire flight of stairs. Okay, so maybe that's a bit far-fetched, but it's what I think every time I'm about to go up or down some stairs.

«When I said, 'my foot is slipping,' your love, O LORD, supported me.»

Psalm 94:18

Recently, though, I've been working on this phobia of mine. I've started looking up more, and I can even have conversations while on the stairs. Hey, this is an improvement for me! But I still have to hold on to that rail. Without it, I would never be able to look up. It guides me and supports me.

Ya know, God is a lot like that rail. The rail is there for you to hold on to; it's there to keep you walking. And so is God. Hold on to God when you're freaking out. Hold on to God when you're scared, lean on God when you need support. If you keep holding on, you'll get through. All stairs end at some point.

«Cast all your anxiety on him because he cares for you.»

1 Peter 5:7

Fail Will

#25 Failure to

I love watching little kids play sports. They are clueless and loving it. And with a little knowledge mixed with imagination, you can piece together the futures of these children.

I remember this one kid and his mom. Cute kid, and you could tell she was a very loving mom. She would do anything for her son, and actually, she pretty much did everything for her son. When he would get a kids' meal, he would dig in the sack straight after the toy. He would grab it and try to open it, and after maybe two half-effort tugs, she would take it and open it for him. When he put his shoes on and would try to place the end of each lace in a loop to make a bow, she would kneel down and say, "*Here, let Mommy help.*" He would go play on the playground, and as soon as he would have to put forth any effort, she would boost him up the rest of the way.

Well, this little boy was finally old enough for T-ball. It was his first game ever and his turn to hit. He took his stance, lined up the bat and the ball, and swung with all of his might, totally missing everything. All the kids laughed because, hey, that's what kids do. He took aim again and with a mighty swing, the ball fell to the ground two feet in front of the tee. A kid picked up the ball and touched him, and he was out.

The boy ran off the field crying. He was devastated. He had never failed. He was so sheltered from the world that he had never had the chance to push himself. Mommy was always there to do it for him. He didn't know the struggle it takes to win, to reach new heights, to accomplish anything.

Make You a Failure

If you never fail, you never stretch yourself to be more than you are. You never learn that there are many ways to solve a single problem. Without failure, you will never discover the cure for cancer. Without failure, man would have never walked on the moon. Without failure, we would still be riding horses to town, sitting around in the dark, hoping that we could get to the closest tree before our bladder exploded. Failures are the hurdles of greatness. Each failure is a brick that builds the foundation of a huge victory. The next time you try something, go big. Because if it's worth doing, it's worth doing in a large way. And if you are going to fail, fail big.

Consider it pure joy, my brothers, whenever you face trials of many kinds, because you know that the testing of your faith develops perseverance. Perseverance must finish its work so that you may be mature and complete, not lacking anything.

James 1:2–4

ME: Hahahaha ... you are Princess Grace, aren't you? Hahahaha.

HER: Shut up, dork. Your #43 moment was pretty stupid too.

ME: Owwwww! Aghhhh!
CRACK!

Tough Lessons
in Tennis and Life

by Brooke

#24

My ankle was broken. Not sprained, not rolled, but B-R-O-K-E-N. And it hurt like nothing I'd ever felt before. How did I do it, you ask? (I'm going to pretend you asked.) I was out playing tennis with my family. We would go out every weekend during the summer and play for hours. We had tons of tennis balls so we didn't have to stop every few minutes to run and pick up the only tennis ball we had. Well, we were playing and the tennis balls were all over because we hadn't stopped to pick them up yet. And my dad hit a killer shot that I thought was going to be in but wound up landing out. I didn't care, though, and went for it anyway. In running for the ball that was out, I stepped on one of the rogue tennis balls and *!CRACK!* went my ankle. I stood on it for a split second before the pain came rushing to my whole body. Then I yelled. Then I fell. Then I cried. Real heroic, eh?

After that experience it took me years to get back onto a tennis court. I had a distaste for tennis after six weeks on crutches and even more time in a cast. Then I finally decided to give it another try. After that many years off the court, it was like I was starting all over again. Before the break, I could serve it wherever I wanted. After the break and all that time, I had to try to remember how to serve. As I stepped on the court, my love for the game came back to me almost immediately, and I was sad that I had taken so much time off from it. I was sad that because of that decision, I was now a beginner again in skill level.

I learned a lot from this painful experience. I learned that you don't need to go for balls that bounce out. I learned that you need to make sure you know where you're stepping and where you're going. And I learned that one bad experience, no matter how painful, shouldn't keep someone from doing what they love. Get back on the court, but watch your step!

"AND THE GOD OF ALL GRACE,
WHO CALLED YOU TO HIS ETER-
NAL GLORY IN CHRIST, AFTER
YOU HAVE SUFFERED A LITTLE
WHILE, WILL HIMSELF RESTORE
YOU AND MAKE YOU STRONG,
FIRM AND STEADFAST."

1 PETER 5:10

#23
Beep, Beep, Beep . . . Snooze

Ah, the best invention ever made and the most annoying one ever made . . . the snooze button.

When that alarm goes off the first time, what a glorious delight to have nine more minutes of sleep. Then how you despise the second ring because nine minutes just isn't enough. So begins the process. Within an instant you calculate, *I have to leave the house at 8:30, and if I skip eating and showering, that buys me 30 minutes, so that equals 3 more snoozes and my alarm was set early, so that's 2 more. So I have 5 total snoozes before I have to get up.*

Then you spend the next 45 minutes sleeping in nine-minute blocks of time. It's enough to drive you nuts, and I am proof that it does! I play this twisted head game with myself every morning. I use my cell as my alarm, and it's on an eight-minute cycle. It fits perfectly in my hand so that the snooze button is right at my thumb. I don't even have to look . . . beep—thumb. It's automatic.

Here is my question. Why don't we set our alarm clocks forward 45 minutes and have that count as prime sleep time instead of trying to hold on to one more wink of sleep snooze by snooze? I just don't get it.

Well, yeah, I do get it. Every night I lie to myself and think that tomorrow I am going to start the day off right. I am going to get up early, spend time with God, and not have to rush around like a madman trying to get out the door.

And when morning comes . . . beep—thumb . . . and the rationalization and justification begins. Every morning I rationalize that if I sleep eight more minutes, then I will be more awake when I spend time with God, so it will be better time. I justify that I don't really need to bathe. After all, I did two mornings ago. I start convincing myself how just four more eight-minute tracts of time will make everything okay.

This is what we do with our God-life. If someone is rude to us and ticks us off, we just write them off. Snooze. We can justify it to ourselves by saying that we are children of God and we shouldn't be treated that way. Yeah, and you know what? That's their issue. Your issue is forgiveness and turning the other cheek.

We go too far and cross some physical lines . . . snooze. We get a little over the line with our crush, we justify that we are testing our strength, and since we stopped and didn't go any further, God is proud and knows how committed we are.

C'mon. Stop rationalizing your me-centered choices. When something comes around and you feel totally justified and can rationalize how your decision is the right one—even though it may hurt someone else or may not be God's decision—get a grip on the head game you are playing with yourself and go bounce the other way.

In Exodus 3 God told Moses what he needed to do. Moses made excuses and rationalized to the all-knowing Creator why he had picked the wrong guy. Go check it out. I found about five excuses that Moses threw out at God. But when Moses finally gave up the not-me attitude and just did what God said, it changed the world. When you stop dropping the roadblocks of rationalization about your anti-God decisions then you will be ready to have heaven opened up and dumped on you.

Justification . . . buzz . . . snooze . . . get up and get moving!

Too bad they don't make alarm clocks

that snooze for
random amounts
of time so you never

know

when it's

going

to go off

again . . .

hmm . . .

Deodorant

Have you ever been sitting in class, acting like you're awake, when all of a sudden you catch a whiff of a nasal ninja dead set on melting the lining of your nostrils? Somebody needs to be arrested by the BO Patrol. There's no escaping it. You go into self-preservation mode and pull your shirt over your nose so you can suck in air through your makeshift funk filter. You secure the edges and take a deep breath . . . ABORT! ABORT! It's you. You are the aroma assassin.

You put your shirt down and think, *Maybe no one noticed.*

They noticed. If you smelled it, so did they. Your only hope is that they can't pinpoint the perpetrator.

You are counting down the ticks before you can go make a pit repair . . . and . . . go!

You take off and isolate yourself so you won't be discovered. Now the dilemma. Deodorant or soap?

D-O for Your B-O

Deodorant is our quick-fix friend. We should have some handy at all times for those messy moments that sneak up on us. But there is a downside. Deodorant doesn't remove anything. It only covers the cause. Don't get me wrong, that's good. But it's just a quick fix that will help keep us going.

That's what Proverbs 17 is talking about when it says, "He who covers an offense promotes love, but whoever repeats the matter separates close friends." If someone does something that totally stinks but you cover it up and say, *Don't worry about it. I forgive you,* then you are promoting love. You are covering up the odor with some holy roll-on.

Soap It Up!

The true funk fighter is good ol' soap and water. That is what washes away those beastly bacteria that cause body odor and gives you a fresh, clean start. Take a whiff of that . . . pure olfactory exhilaration.

vs Soap

Check out John 13:5–14 for the whole story

Cleaning it away is what *keeps* you fresh. Jesus laid this out when he was washing the disciples' feet. He got to Peter, and Peter was like, *"No way. You're not washing my feet."* And Jesus was like, *"You can't be a part of me if you don't let me wash your feet."* And Peter said, *"Hey, then give me the super-soaker cycle and get my head and body too."*

Jesus had to break it way down for Peter and remind him that it's about the feet. Your bod is clean, but you gotta keep your feet clean.

I'll break it down even more for you. If you are a follower of Christ, you have gone through the Holy Spirit Hand Wash, and you are clean. One time. No need for do-over's. Now it's all about the touch-ups. You have to keep the sin off. When you do get some on you, repent and get it clean again. If not, it's that grime that will keep you from God's glory.

So let's review our heavenly hygiene:

- ☑ deodorant: to cover up and forgive someone when they've done something that stinks, keeping the relationship polished and pretty
- ☑ soap: to cleanse you and keep things nice and shiny between you and God

Now go out into the world of smudge, smog, and smlurp and apply deodorant on others—and keep yourself soaped up and clean.

Not everyone on the hockey team was excited to have a girl playing. One guy, Jimmy, wanted to teach me a lesson. The lesson was that girls don't belong on the ice rink playing hockey. What he didn't know is that he taught me a completely different lesson altogether.

I was the only girl on the guys' ice hockey team in my high school. To say I was extremely nervous for my first practice is an understatement. I got to the rink early and was told by some guy that the girls' dressing room was the second door on the left. I thanked him, went to the second door, and quickly realized he had sent me to the utility closet. Great way to start things.

I got all suited up in all of my pads. Hockey pads are not only expensive but amazingly protective. They have to be, considering how rough the sport can be. My legs were shaking so badly as I took my first step onto the ice that I almost lost my balance. Midway through the practice I was calming down. The guys on the team were so great; they were taking time to show me tricks and helping me. They had taken me under their wings, and I was the "little sister" of all the guys. Well, not all of them. This is where Jimmy comes in.

Jimmy the Jerk • by the Ice Hockey Queen Brooke

#21

Practice was ending and the coach was calling us in to wrap it up. We had just finished scrimmaging and were all panting from exhaustion. As I skated in, my head was down and I was unaware that Jimmy was skating at me full speed. When he checked me as hard as he could, I went flying. My stick went one way, one of my gloves went the other way, and I went sliding across the rink. When I looked up, I saw that the whole team was skating over to me. They were all worried and wanted to know if I was okay. And I was. I was actually great! My pads made it so I didn't feel a thing! I had taken a serious hit that would have been illegal in any game and was still standing—well, I was lying down at the moment, but I got back up and was standing.

This is going to happen to us as Christians. We are going to meet people who don't like us being on God's team. As a team, we are responsible for taking care of each other and helping each other up when we've been hit. People and circumstances will come at us when we're at our weakest or when we're not looking, and they will hit us with all they have. But check it out. God gives us the pads to protect us. He gives us the helmet of salvation, the breastplate of righteousness, the belt of truth, the shield of faith, the gospel of peace fitted and ready on our feet, and our sword the Bible. And if you don't know what all of that means, you need to go to Ephesians 6:10–20 and get a little knowledge of how all of this works.

When the attack comes, yeah, we'll feel the hit, but it won't destroy us. Our God-gear will protect us, our teammates will help us up, and our team will only get stronger.

Did I Learn

by Brooke

College is awesome.

Seriously, it was one of the most amazing experiences of my life. It's one of the first times in your life when you make all the decisions. You get to call the shots, and you say what goes. If you want to schedule it so your first class of the day doesn't start until noon, then do it! If you want to study all night at a coffeehouse, then do it! It's your call.

While I loved just about everything that had to do with college and college life, there was one thing that I couldn't stand. It wasn't dorm rooms, it wasn't cafeteria food, and it wasn't all of the extra reading. It was my math class. Now, I've never really liked math, but I *had* to go in high school, so there was no avoiding it. But college is different. In some college classes, the professor doesn't make you go. That's right, if you don't want to go to a class . . . you don't have to go! So seeing as math was a class that I never understood and never even cared about, I wasn't a regular. I would find other things to do, like go to lunch, hang out with friends, or even work on homework for other classes. The first time I skipped the class, I felt horrible. Then I got used to the idea. Eventually I was skipping math class without a second thought. Second thoughts are underrated, though—especially around finals time.

I decided to go to every math class the two weeks before finals. I thought that this would be enough time to get back into the groove and that I'd be fine for the final exam. The classes that I went to were almost all review from the whole semester. This would have been sweet if I had known anything they were talking about. How could I review a class that I didn't even go to? I did my best to cram

That? #20

and figure out the review sheet. I wasn't feeling too great about this final.

When I showed up for the final, I had a horrible feeling in my gut. No matter how much I had crammed or how hard I had tried to pay attention the previous two weeks, I still felt lost. I had missed a whole semester and was now about to be tested on it. If you've ever gone into a test knowing that you were about to fail, you know what I was going through. It's a horrible feeling to know the negative outcome before it happens. Unfortunately, I couldn't have had a more accurate gut feeling about this test. I failed my math final.

You can't pass the test if you don't go to class. The whole point of class is to gather the necessary knowledge for the final exam. Think of the Bible as your way to gather necessary knowledge. It's the ultimate textbook. In your Bible study groups or youth groups, you can study the Word so you understand God's messages. "Let me understand the teaching of your precepts; then I will meditate on your wonders." This is a class where failing the test will result in more than just having to repeat the class. Use my experience for your own benefit; go to class and don't put off studying. This A is worth it.

Psalm 119:27

"I have hidden your word in my heart that I might not sin against you." Psalm 119:11

"I delight in your decrees; I will not neglect your word." Psalm 119:16

Just go read all of Psalm 119. You'll get the hint.

Are You a Christian?

Well, are you a Christian? If you are, how could I tell?

Could I tell you're a Christian because your bumper sticker says so . . . or because you waved to someone to let them in front of you while driving?

Could I tell you're a Christian because you're a member of a Christian club . . . or because you spend your weekends helping those in need?

Could I tell you're a Christian because you're wearing a shirt that says you are . . . or because you donate clothing to shelters?

Could I tell you're a Christian because of the big silver cross you wear around your neck . . . or because you treat everyone like they are made of gold?

Could I tell you're a Christian because you've memorized the Word in your head . . . or because you've memorized the Word in your heart?

Could I tell you're a Christian because you say that you are . . . or because you live every day for God?

Are you a Christian?

_____

_____

_____

If you are . . . how could I tell?

_____

_____

_____

_____

_____

Cheater Cheater

Pumpkin Eater!

Have you ever cheated at a game? Maybe you've played the game so many times that you know how to win it. Maybe it's a game where you find a way to cheat so no one knows. At hide-and-seek, do you peek while you're counting and everyone is finding a place to hide? Do you deal from the bottom when playing cards? Do you abuse the rules so they work best for you?

How about school? Have you ever cheated at school? Maybe you spent all night watching TV and didn't study. Maybe your best friend is a genius at math, and she happens to be really nice too. Maybe she owes you a favor, so you ask if you can see her homework. Or maybe you don't even ask. Maybe your eyes wander on quizzes. Maybe.

Have you ever cheated on a boyfriend? Have you ever cheated on a girlfriend? What they don't know can't hurt them, right? Maybe it was your one shot to be with that guy. Maybe you've always liked that girl, and now that you're dating someone, she's interested. Maybe it didn't mean anything because you didn't love the fling. It was just a one-time thing. Maybe.

All of these words can be found in the thesaurus for the words *cheat* or *cheater*:

burn, con, crook, deceive, defraud, double-cross, dupe, mislead, rip off, scam, swindle, trick, victimize, false, two-faced, hustle, faithless, and treacherous.

In case you're not a word wizard, none of those words are good in any way. Same goes with cheating.

"Good people are guided by their honesty; treacherous people are destroyed by their dishonesty."

Proverbs 11:3 NLT

Everything in life works like a wave. I'm sitting here in Tybee Island, Georgia, just feet from the crashing waves. I'm tuned in. I'm really listening. Sometime when you have a chance, listen to nothing but waves. They are loud as they rush toward you—strong and unstoppable—and then for no reason, they seem to retreat. It's as though they are pulled away. Back and forth they go, Earth's emotional roller coaster. It pretty much sums up life.

You rush toward your education. Your college plan is a sure thing. Then your career choice . . . not so sure after all as you retreat into your workplace rut. That guy you are so sure is Mr. Right (okay, so it's the fifth time you've been so sure) goes *poof*! He just evaporates before your very eyes! Prayer life? You rush toward God every Monday just like a new diet. You promise to spend quality time each day reading the Word. You vow to spend more time in prayer—not

The waves of death swirled about me;
the torrents of destruction overwhelmed me.

2 Samuel 22:5

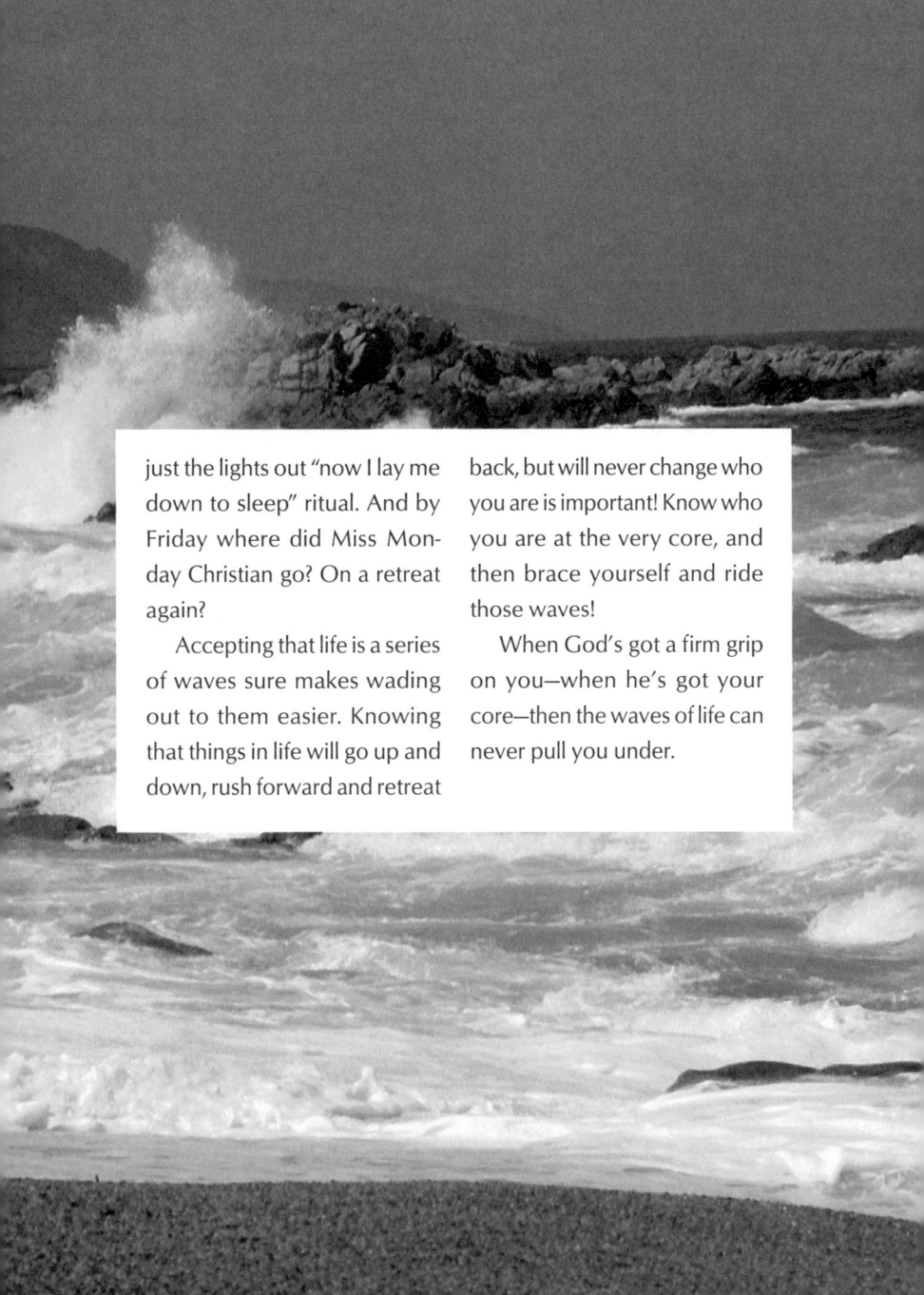

just the lights out "now I lay me down to sleep" ritual. And by Friday where did Miss Monday Christian go? On a retreat again?

Accepting that life is a series of waves sure makes wading out to them easier. Knowing that things in life will go up and down, rush forward and retreat back, but will never change who you are is important! Know who you are at the very core, and then brace yourself and ride those waves!

When God's got a firm grip on you—when he's got your core—then the waves of life can never pull you under.

He reached down from on high and took hold of me.

2 Samuel 22:17

#16   First Impressions

How do people see you? When they first look at you or have contact with you, what do they think about you? Well, it's time to find out.

You are going to be your own lab rat. Grab a bud and hit the mall, the beach, or anywhere you have a safe zone for contacting some people.

It is widely known that people who carry clipboards are doing important work. Lab coats give you prestige and power. Want teachers to treat you with respect? Try wearing a white lab coat to school and asking them to call you Doctor.

Give your lab partner a clipboard, paper, and pen, and if you can get a white lab coat, that would be extra suave. This person will henceforth be known as the "scientist." The person who is being examined will be known as the "lab rat." And the random person being asked for their observation and opinion will be known as the "test subject."

Follow these steps for your experiment:

I.   Position the lab rat in convenient view for observation.
II. Approach a test subject and say: "Hello, my name is _____ (make up a good scientific name) and I am doing a scientific study on first impressions. If you don't mind, please look at that person (point to your lab rat) and give me your first impression of him/her."
III. When the lab rat sees the scientist point in their direction, the lab rat should walk toward the test subject, simply say, "Hi, my name is _____" (first name only), and then walk away.
IV. The scientist should then ask the subject to give several words to describe their first impression, like nice, rude, aggressive, shy, smart. And then ask if the first impression in general was positive, negative, or "eh, whatever."
V.   Record data.

When you've gathered data from several subjects, sit down as scientist and lab rat and see if the answers you received are the ones you thought you would.

Bonus: If you wanted to change people's first impressions of you, what are some things that you could do?

Extra Bonus: Those things you think you could change—change them, and then run the test again to see if it worked.

Extra Extra Bonus: Change random things about you and guess what impression the changes would make. Run the test again to see if you were right.

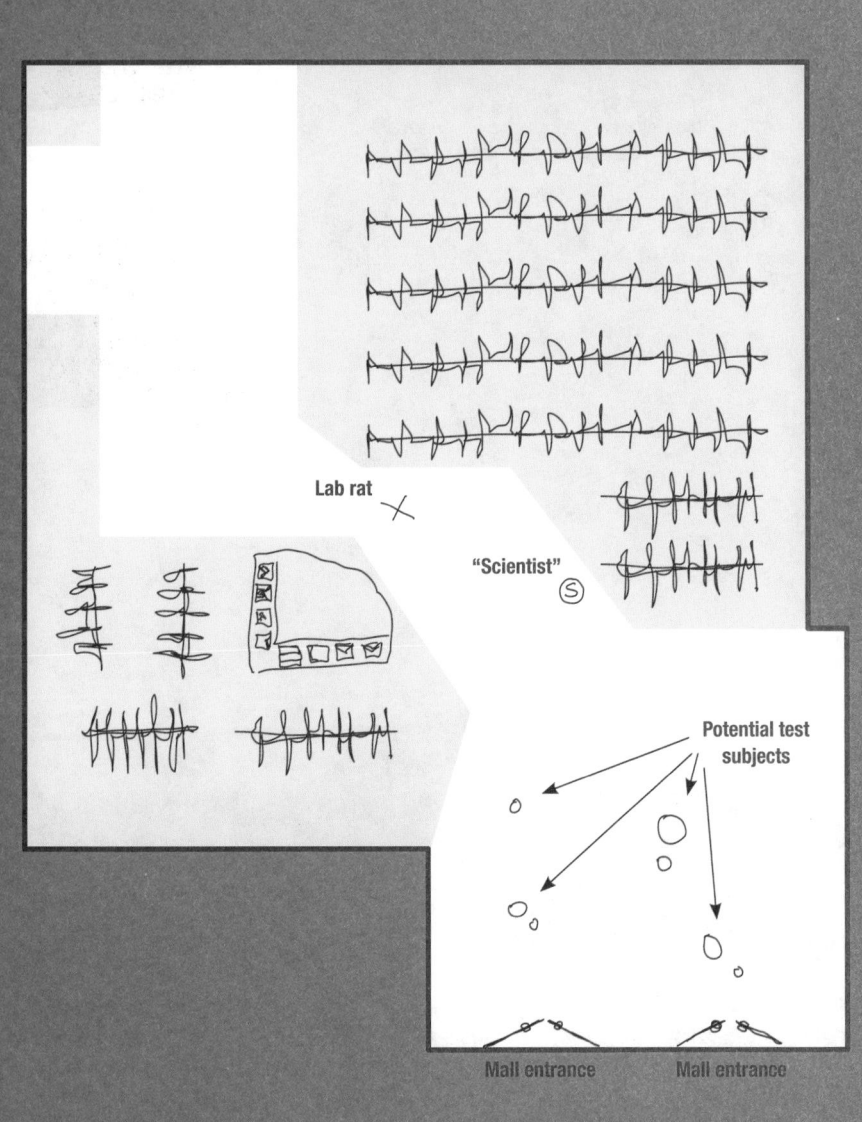

Top view of a typical mall entrance.

I had my cowboy hat on and my boots with my pants tucked in 'em. I had a bandana around my neck and my BB gun in my hand. I was not a seven-year-old boy. I was the sheriff. And I was here to catch some bad guys.

I snuck out the back door of the house because I knew they were watching the front. I ran and did a dive roll behind a tree. I crawled on the ground behind the rosebush. I sprinted behind the stack of wood. I sat there catching my breath and getting my plan together.

I stuck my gun over the top of the wood and gave them a warning shot. There was no movement, but I knew they were hiding in the green Plymouth sitting in the driveway. No doubt about it. I had to do something. We were running low on supplies, and winter was coming. I decided to do the unexpected and rush 'em.

I leaned against the wood, said a prayer, and then walked out toward the gang, letting the muzzle of my rifle lead the way. And I started firing.

I could see their faces through the windshield. And with each face I would pull the trigger and re-cock for the next one. BBs were flying like rain. I was taking them out as fast as they would show themselves.

I fired 1, 2, 3, 4, 5 shots. Then 6 . . . 7 . . . and on the 7th my world fell apart. On 7 the windshield of the Plymouth that the bad guys had been hiding in shattered into a thousand little pieces. I dropped

my gun and took off, running around screaming. I don't think I ever saw John Wayne do that, but then again, I never saw John Wayne shoot out his dad's windshield.

I was shocked, horrified, and totally baffled. Later my dad explained to me—after he "explained" some other things to me—that one little BB wasn't enough to shatter a windshield, but each one put a little chip, a little weak spot in the glass, and seven little weak spots put together were enough to destroy the whole thing.

You know, that man had a lot of wisdom in those words. Because that's the way it is with little sins. Not our big ones. Our baby ones. We tell a "little white lie," we ignore the new kid, we ask for water at a restaurant and then get a soda. None of these will shatter your world. But each tiny little thing leaves a chip, a weakness. And when they build up enough, your life will start crumbling, and you'll be shocked and baffled.

That's like in Proverbs 6:10–11 where it says, "A little sleep, a little slumber, a little folding of the hands to rest—and poverty will come on you like a bandit and scarcity like an armed man."

God is not anti-naptime. He is anti-compromise. He is anti–letting the enemy get even a small BB hole in your life. Be strong. God gave you the Holy Spirit, so when you are weak, he is strong. Don't compromise on the little stuff, and don't shoot out any windshields.

Don't sweat the small stuff and don't pet the sweaty stuff.

A Message to My Children

For many life is harsh
It seems good luck passed them by
Some overcome by getting a job
While others would rather die.

This message is to the two of you
That do not want to work
Moving home with your parents
Is not a viable perk.

So if it gets down to grown children starving
Your parents will be so sad
So don't bother to waste your energy
Writing for cash from dear old Dad.

Frank Lookadoo
July 2004

**For this reason a man will leave his father
and mother and be united to his wife, and
they will become one flesh.**

Genesis 2:24

Okay, I definitely see a couple of things going on here. I mean, dear ol' Dad was kinda vague if you ask me, but after doing a little study of the poem, I am starting to feel like he doesn't want us living in his house anymore. It seems to me as if he is hinting at the fact that we are on our own, especially now that I am married. Yeah, sure, Dad, pick this issue to get all biblical about. I guess that whole *Failure to Launch* syndrome is not welcome here. That's okay, I can take it.

The second thing I think he is alluding to is that we don't have a piggy bank left at his house. Call me naïve, but I am pretty sure he is saying that the cash pool has dried up and we are, again, on our own.

In that case, let me talk to you, dear reader. Please, please, please go buy my books. I know, it's not very manly to beg, but I am begging. Our safety net has been cut and I have no other option.

Our conservative estimates are that every book sold has been read by about three people. That is great. The message is getting out there, and that is way cool, but that doesn't help us stay out of my dad's house. When I go to an event and fifteen people have read my book and only one copy was bought, my father starts getting really nervous. He knows that I get nothing off of rereads and pass-alongs. So for my father's sake, help an old man live out his retirement years without breaking out into a sweat every time a moving van goes by his house. Buy my books. When someone wants to borrow yours, tell them where they can get one of their very own. This will let my father relax, and it will help Emily and me stay away from his guest room. Who knows? I may even take him out to dinner . . . and pay this time.

Oh, and if you haven't noticed by now, I like to ask a lot of questions, and I like it even more when you answer. The stuff I write is made to be used. Don't be afraid to write in the books, answer the questions, dog-ear the corners, heck, even rip out the pages you want to take with you. (From your own book. Not from someone else's book or one sitting in the store.) I am a big fan of doodles and underlines. Make the book yours. Put your thoughts down. I do that all the time. That's a huge reason I don't let anyone borrow my books. They become like journals to me, full of my own ideas and secrets that I don't want anyone to know. Do that with the books you get from me. Make them your hiding place for what you really feel. You'll be amazed at what happens when you get your vibe out there on paper. It will connect what you read with your life, your heart, the real you. Have fun, get messy, and commence to doodling.

If you need some help, here is a list of my other books:

Dateable: Are You? Are They?
The Dateable Rules
The Dirt on Sex
The Dirt on Drugs
The Dirt on Breaking Up
The Hardest 30 Days of Your Life

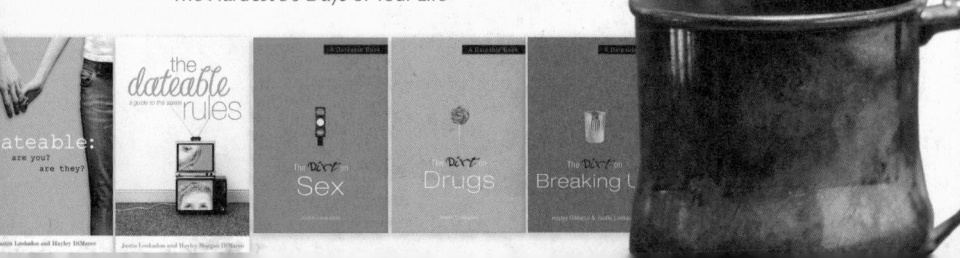

Musk Ox Man

"Be strong and let us fight bravely for our people and the cities of our God. The LORD will do what is good in his sight."

2 Samuel 10:12

I have a new favorite animal. I know in #86 I told you it was the duck-billed platypus. Well, I changed my mind. Yep, the DBP has been snubbed by my new fave, which is now officially the *Ovibos moschatus,* better know as the musk ox.

A musk ox looks like a cross between a bison and a water buffalo, with a hint of woolly mammoth. Shrink all that down to a pseudo-miniature size, and there you have it. Can't get the visual, then google it.

I caught a glimpse of some of these guys in Alaska. They were so cute, in an evolutionarily-stunted kinda way. But don't let their cuteness fool you. They aren't weak little links in the food chain. Hey, the Ice Age couldn't even kill these things.

And let me tell you the coolest thing about these animals. When trouble comes and an underfed carnivore in need of some red meat starts stalking the musk ox buffet, the herd forms a defensive circle. They put the old, young, female, and weak in the middle of the circle, and the strong stand shoulder to shoulder with horns and hard heads ready to attack whatever is daring enough or stupid enough to try to break through.

Think about it—isn't that the way we're supposed to live? Side by side we stand in strength. Defending God's laws and principles and protecting those who can't defend themselves—even if it costs us our own life! You read about men like this in the Bible, but you don't really hear much about similar dudes these days. In fact, just like the musk ox, men like that are dangerously close to extinction!

Yeah, you heard me—*men like that!* Men who stand up for what they believe, who don't prey on the weak but defend them. Who treat people right, and that means ladies! They are gentle, yet strong—not bullies, but not pushovers—not pansies, but not jerks! Real men are what I'm calling for here—real godly men. Men who aren't afraid to take on the enemy, but not at the cost of harming those they should be protecting. If you don't get the visual here, *don't* google it. Just start reading the Word.

Let's step up, guys—let's learn from these prehistoric creatures (the furry animals, not the Bible fellas).

Keep it simple, keep it strong, and keep this breed alive.

#12

No Ordinary Puppy Love

Emily works with the 8th-grade girls at our church. I've met most of them, and they're all pretty cool, but this one girl blew me away. She was cute, thin, with long dark hair, and she had the best laugh. I noticed her when she was in the car, but in a room full of people you probably wouldn't notice her. She wasn't the loudest or tallest. She didn't draw the most attention. Probably not the kid who would be voted "most likely to change the world," but she did.

She was listening to the radio, and they were talking about some dude who was real sick. Bad sick. And he wished he had a little Chihuahua that could sit in his lap and keep him company. He talked about how alone and isolated he felt.

As she listened, her heart broke. It broke even more when her little Chihuahua walked into the room and hopped into her lap. Tears started flowing down her cheeks, and she knew what she had to do.

This is a listening to God thing.

She called the radio station and offered to give her dog to the guy. She wanted it to be totally on the sly so he would not know who gave it to him. She wanted the guy to just enjoy the dog without feeling he owed anybody anything.

It happened. The guy got the dog, and that was the end of the story . . . until . . .

It had been a couple of weeks since she had given up the dog when she got a call from the radio station. They said she needed to come

> *Don't let anyone look down on you because you are young, but set an example for the believers in speech, in life, in love, in faith and in purity.*
>
> *1 Timothy 4:12*

back down there. They wouldn't tell her why. She just had to come down.

She got her mom to take her to the station. She was in for the surprise of her life.

See, the radio station had told all its listeners what this anonymous 8th grade girl had done, how she gave up her dog for some man she would never meet. Someone else was listening to this story, and he arranged the same kind of thing. He called the radio station, and without revealing who he was, he gave this young lady a $1,000 gift certificate to Best Buy. She was able to go buy a computer that helps her do homework and, of course, stay connected with her pals.

You think you can't make a difference because you're too young? This 8th grade girl started a chain of events that changed lives, including hers.

There was a man with no money who wanted a dog.

There was a girl who had no money but had a dog.

There was another man who had no dog but had money.

Because of this one girl, a man got a dog, she got a computer, and the other guy got the huge satisfaction of giving the girl something she couldn't get for herself.

What are you doing to make a difference?

Oh, Deer

I was down in the Hill Country of Texas riding my motorcycle. Oh, it was perfect. About 80 degrees, sunshine, low traffic—perfect. I had my trip planned out exactly so that I could get back to where I was staying before the sun went down.

As I turned onto my final leg, I realized I had miscalculated my time. The sun had set, it was already dark, and I had a 15-mile ride down the most dangerous road of the trip ahead of me. It was up and down, S-turn after S-turn, with rocks and gravel on the road. I didn't know this road, but I did know that deer rule this part of Texas. When the sun goes down, the deer come out. And I'm not a smart man, but I do know that a deer could be a downer if it jumped in front of a motorcycle.

I set out on this dangerous stretch of highway and started talking with God. I said, "God, you made your furry little animals so you can control them. Keep all your critters out of my way." And then I decided to help him. I would honk my horn for three seconds at a time. That way I could warn the animal kingdom that I was coming through. On the third honk, out of nowhere some little creature darted into the road. And instead of choosing any other part of this road, this fur ball picked the few inches my tires were riding on. He ran right in front of me and stopped.

I knew I was dead. This was going to wreck my world.

I prepared for the worst, and I felt a quick *thump*

> So then, let us not be like others, who are asleep, but let us be alert and self-controlled.
>
> 1 Thessalonians 5:6

thump. My tires didn't sway. The bike didn't swerve. I just kept on going. Immediately I heard God say, *"I didn't need your help. If you want me to control my critters, I will, but I don't need you to help me by honking."*

I said, *"Okay, what do you need me to do?"*

God said, *"Stay alert and stay focused. Nothing more. Nothing less. Stay alert and stay focused."*

I drove the rest of the way very alert and very focused. And you know, God took care of me and controlled his critters. In fact, I had to pass through this one small town. And I think, just as a reminder that God was in control, when I went by the town post office, there was a deer standing in the driveway waiting for me to go past. And when I did, he trotted across the road.

God wants you to do two things. Stay alert and stay focused. Stay alert to any dangers and problems that may be thrown at you. And stay focused on him by digging into his Word for direction. Stay alert and stay focused.

I hope no animals were hurt during the writing of this devotional.

Oh, quit whining! Whatever it was got up and ran away. . . . The *jerk* . . . uh, I mean, cute little furry God's creature . . . amen.

*Names of all the animals have been changed to protect the innocent.

Seed. Water. Grow.

This dude was coaching girls' basketball in Kansas. The team had made it to the playoffs, and he was sitting in the gym getting prepped. His star player walked across the court, sat down, and said, "Coach, can I talk to you?"

He was so zoned on what he was doing that he said, "Yeah, sure," and didn't even look up from what he was doing.

She took a deep breath, exhaled slowly, and let it rip: "Coach, I think your life's a joke." He stopped and his focus snapped to her. She continued, "You coach basketball, you teach, but you don't live for anything. It's just kinda pathetic. If you ever want to change that and start living for something, then I am here and would love to talk to you about it." She got up and went into the dressing room.

He was hot! He could feel his ears getting red, and he was ticked. She zinged him and then ran into the girls' locker room where he couldn't go.

Two nights later he was sitting at home, and he was still ticked. And the more he thought about it, the madder he got. Not because of what she had said but because he knew she was right.

He tried to watch TV. He tried to get it out of his mind, but nothing was working. Finally he hit the remote, turned off the show, and got on his knees and cried out to God. He didn't really know what he was doing because he'd never really talked to God before. But that night his life was changed.

Now he is a youth pastor at one of the largest churches in Oklahoma—all because a teenage girl planted a seed. She didn't pound him over the head and demand a decision. She did what God wanted her to do. She dropped a seed into her coach and walked away. She didn't water it, grow it, nothing.

Listen, you don't have to convert anyone. Just start tossing out seeds. Like it says in 1 Corinthians 3:6–8, "I planted the seed, Apollos watered it, but God made it grow. So neither he who plants nor he who waters is anything, but only God, who makes things grow. The man who plants and the man who waters have one purpose, and each will be rewarded according to his own labor." Hey, you never know. You might be the one who has to add a little water so that the seed will pop up and start growing. Take the pressure to convert every person off of yourself, and quit making lame excuses as to why you don't say anything. Do your part and let God do his.

Getting Muddy

Do you have anything that makes you kinda giggly when you think about it being yours? I know, the fellas reading this would never admit to getting "giggly." Hey guys, I'm secure in my manhood and I'm not afraid to admit that I do.

Every time I open my garage, I smile, because there sits a 1972 K5 Chevy Blazer. Not one of these weenie Blazers. I'm talking big boy size. Four-wheel drive, six-inch lift, thirty-six-inch tires, three-ton winch on the front, fully convertible and fully restored. Arrrrrrrrrrrrrgh! (In your best pirate voice!)

When I first got that little he-toy, I took it out in the woods to find some mud I could play in, and mud I found. I was spinning and turning and just going crazy. And then I came to "the pit." A perfect spot for my baby to play. A pit of water and mud, and it was calling our names. We took off across it, spinning, blowing, and going. When we were about to come out on the other side, all of a sudden all forward movement stopped. Bump!

What I did not realize was that this perfect little hole was a place where someone had been digging out and removing dirt. That meant that the entry was a smooth slope, the exit . . . not so much. The exit was a three-foot step that my front tires slammed into.

The truck stopped and all four wheels were spinning. I threw it into reverse to try to go the other way. Nothing. Backward. Forward. Backward. Forward. I was stuck.

I opened the door of my truck, and instead of having to stretch to reach the ground like I normally do, the ground was all the way up to the door. Whoa.

I'm not a smart fella, but I knew I needed help. I called for some.

I called some friends and they came to the rescue. John hooked up his Toyota 4Runner to the Blazer and started cranking his winch to pull me out. I just sat there in the Blazer . . . not moving. I looked up and there he was, getting closer and closer to the pit. He was trying to help me and I was dragging him into the pit, and you guessed it . . . stuck.

This is what the Word is talking about when it says, "Brothers, if someone is caught in a sin, you who are spiritual should restore him gently. But watch yourself, or you also may be tempted." You may be helping someone or reaching out to them and doing it on the up and up, but it may end up dragging you down before you know it.

It's okay to go into the muck and try to help others get their lives unstuck. But make sure you don't go alone and you stay connected to solid Christians who can help you while you're helping others. Stay connected. And be careful.

3 Small Lessons from God

more observations by Emily

Justin always has said that God gave him the gift of speaking so that he could help change people, and he does. Writing, on the other hand, doesn't come so easily for him. Those of us who are near him each day and have to watch this agonizing journey each time he writes a book sometimes question why God would ask him to write. To be honest, it's a painful ritual for Justin and a hard one for those who love him to witness. But Justin always answers us by saying that God uses his writing to change him. God uses his speaking to change others and his writing to change him. Hmmm.

This time around I thought, *Okay, God, I guess this is gonna be another one of those times. This time please give me something to do to keep me busy enough that I don't focus on Justin. Please use this time while Justin's writing to change me too.* And he has, but as God often does, he chose a way I could have never imagined.

Joe and Caroline are a couple on my street whom I had only met one time prior to February. In February they were finally blessed with the family they'd been longing for. Instant family, that is—they were blessed with triplets! Triplets, triplets, triplets. Cole, Kai, and Carys. If you have never had the privilege of being around a newborn for longer than an hour, I encourage you to experience their demands for twenty-four hours, then multiply that by three, but remember, there is still only one mom and one dad. It makes for dreadfully long days and dreadfully long nights. Every three hours the babies must eat. One feeding can take upwards of an hour, which doesn't leave very long to prepare for the next round of bottles, diaper changes, clothing changes, and so on. And that's on an easy day—sometimes they cry for no reason and there is no break between the feeds. Other days they need baths in between the feeds. Some days Caroline's only prayer is that she can brush her teeth today—seems simple, but trust me, it isn't. She goes through over twenty-four bottles and diapers a day. The laundry is overwhelming: burp-stained clothes, socks, outfits, washrags, blankets, crib sheets, bibs, not to mention her and Joe's laundry too. Caroline and Joe haven't slept longer than three hours since February 3. They are beyond exhausted, and outnumbered. Their sacrifices never end.

So anyway, Justin hit the road to go write this book. Wanting to be a good charitable Chris-

tian, I decided to call Caroline and volunteer to help her. I was going to pour myself into others so I wouldn't be focusing on Justin. I would help her with feeding the little ones and ease her load. At least that was *my* plan. A couple feeds a week quickly turned into three to four feeds each day, five days a week! It didn't take me long to figure out that this charitable act I was doing was God's way of changing me. Justin and I have been around kids our whole lives; kids' lives are in fact our entire livelihood. And like many other Christians, we've both said that children are God's miracles and heaven-sent. We've *always* said it and we've *always* meant it, but it wasn't until these triplets that I truly understood.

Holding three premature babies every single day gives you a lot of time to just watch. To watch the process, watch every little tiny change. To watch them go from fitting in my hand to making my arms tired because they've gained weight. To see how they can hold their heads up now without my help. To know they recognize you and to wait for the smile to appear as you approach. To be able to distinguish between their individual coos and grunts. And with three of them, there are no breaks. There's always another baby to hold. It's baby after baby after baby.

I guess it took three babies (back-to-back-to-back) for God to make his point: Undeniably, these three babies are nothing shy of a miracle. These three small bundles turned out to be three large lessons from God.

My spirit has been touched profoundly, and I've never felt so loved in my life, because these babies that I hold in my arms are miracles. And so is every one of you reading this now. Each one of you is a miracle, as am I. And if I feel this way just watching three small babies, I can only imagine how God must feel looking down at all of his babies. All of us. For the first time in a very long time, I don't question how much I am loved, and I'm so grateful for God's ultimate sacrifice for me.

"But from everlasting to everlasting the Lord's love is with those who fear him, and his righteousness with their children's children."

Psalm 103:17

#7

A friend of mine named Mark Hall took a

little time out of his Casting Crowns tour

and stopped in to see me during the writing

of *97*. He wanted to drop some wisdom

on you, and I was honored to let him. So

sit back and enjoy the deep ramblings of a

great friend and a twisted mind.

How To Kill a Friendship in 4 Easy Steps

I guess there is an excess of high-quality friends out there. As I watch the students in my group as well as those across the nation, I see some of the best friendships destroyed and tossed away. It seems like a pretty difficult task, so me being the happy helper I am, I wanted to help make it easier to get rid of those unwanted best buds. Follow these four easy steps and I guarantee you will lose your friends in no time.

1. Never deal with the anger—keep packing it in

Focus totally on how you hate the person. Make sure you never assume that the issue is the real problem. Blame the person. If you miss this crucial first step, you might realize that it's really not that big of a deal or that the person didn't even know they hurt you. Accepting this would limit your success in losing your friends.

"Don't let the sun go down while you are still angry" (Ephesians 4:26). I think the reason God said this is because he knows what we do when we lie in bed at night ticked off. You know what I'm talking about. You run through every possible scenario in your mind: When she said *this* I should have said *that*. And then when she said *that* I should have said *this*. And tomorrow if she even says anything to me I'm gonna . . . and you have this argument with somebody who's not even there.

The next morning in class this fantasy foe asks you if she can borrow a pencil, and you stab her in the neck. Whoa, Trigger. You explode and they don't have a clue what just happened. Yeah, God knows you need to get rid of that junk so you don't build it up way bigger than it is—unless, of course, you are trying to lose your friends.

Plan B: If you are looking to keep your friends, deal with each issue as it happens. Let them know what upset you and why. Not in a slamfest kinda way but in a way that lets them know that you really want to be friends. You'll be amazed at how many times they didn't even realize what upset you and they'll feel totally rotten and make it up to you.

2. Never deal with the person—always form a committee

All in favor of creating a committe say "Aye."

Oh yeah, the more people you get involved, the better. If you try to deal with the person directly, you will almost always get the unwanted result of relational restoration. Instead, tell as many people as possible, taking extra care to make the other person look horrible. If you can get these Mad Club members to say bad things about your soon-to-be-ex best friend, that will make the process go even quicker. That way if you're confronted, you get to look shocked and say, "I never said that. Someone else must have."

Plan B: Close Friend Conservation requires doing what Scripture says and going to the person one-on-one. Hey, it's your issue, no one else's. Doing it this way allows you to strengthen your bond without throwing your dirty laundry out there for everyone to see.

Do nothing out of selfish ambition or vain conceit, but in humility consider others better than yourselves. Each of you should look not only to your own interests, but also to the interests of others. Philippians 2:3–4

3. Believe everything you hear—don't worry about the truth

Yeah, this is the Oprah Syndrome. If someone heard it on *Oprah*, then it must be true. Just like if someone tells you that they heard someone say something about you, then yep, it must be true. If you are going to bounce your best buds and keep them gone, you have to believe everything you hear.

Oh, and if you really want to amp up the conflict, conduct your arguments over email and IM. Emails have no voice, no tone. So whatever mood you are in will determine how the email sounds to you. If you are happy, it will sound happy. If you are ticked off, it will sound like an attack.

Plan B: To reverse the unfriend trend, try a little something called discernment. Here's how it works: If you hear something and it's no big deal, then just blow it off. No biggie. If it's a character crusher, then you'll probably want to check out the source. See what is really going on. Remember, they are a friend, but they are also human, and sometimes that means doing and saying some stupid things. Give 'em a chance. Someday you'll need them to do the same for you.

4. Learn to apologize—without apologizing

This is an art and may take some time to master. Some of you are already experts at this, and the rest of you will be there in no time if you follow these tips.

The Explosive "I'm Sorry"

This is the primary unapology. When the person is telling you what you did to hurt them, just blurt out "I'm sorry!" Make sure you are short, a little loud, and rude-sounding. Cutting them off in the middle of their sentence is an added bonus. If you are Advanced Level you can add "Okay, fine" to the "I'm sorry." This will let the person know that you don't agree with them one bit and that you are doing this so later on you can tell everyone, "I don't know why she is so upset—I told her I was sorry."

The "I'm Sorry, *But . . .*"

This is a great way to apologize to someone *while* placing the blame anywhere but on you. The added bonus comes when you can place the blame on the person that you are apologizing to. Also try throwing in some random things you are upset about which are totally unrelated to what's happening. This will let the person know that you were totally justified in your actions, so the apology is really just a formality, and you get to boast about how gracious you are.

The "I'm Sorry" Redirect

This one is not for beginners. For some it will take practice. For others it will come naturally. When you know someone is upset, say something like this: "I'm sorry . . . that you misunderstood me" or "I'm sorry . . . that you took it that way." This will set the other person up so they feel like you are totally genuine, but then you knock them right in the face with the redirect. When used effectively this will let the other person know that you think they are stupid, shallow, immature, and unable to have a simple conversation without messing it up and getting confused.

Plan B: When you know you have upset someone and hurt them, apologize. Take responsibility for what you have done. Use words like, "I know it made you feel stupid when I said . . ." "I see how rude I was to you when I . . ." and "I am sooo sorry." After that, if you need to, you may give a little explanation. Not a *but*, rather a *here's what was happening and I am sorry for letting this affect how I treated you.*

Hey, I don't know about you guys, but I don't have a lot of super-solid friends. I need to do everything possible to keep the ones I have. If you are different and have way too many buds, this will help you get rid of those pesky pals. But if you're like me, you might want to give Plan B a shot. Who knows? You might make some friends for life.

Look-a-doo-dad: When someone apologizes to you, try to get over your own little ticked-off-ness and accept it. Don't shut the person down or say stuff like, "**Yeah, you should feel bad.**" Don't remind them of how rude it was. Just accept it and forgive.

EVOLUTION IS TRUE!

That's right, boys and girls, frogs and squirrels, you heard me. Evolution is true.

First, my little word-loving readers, let me give you the definition of evolution as taught in my comparative anatomy class in college:

evolution = change

So yes, evolution has occurred, does occur, and will occur. Mountains, beaches, forests, they all evolve. People evolve. In fact, in 1750 the English had the tallest average height, busting it out at 5'5. Today the average American is 5'9. Thank you, evolution.

Now let's take a peepski at "the theory of evolution." My college degree is in biology. So from my years of hanging with the bio-world, let me tell you what a theory is. Theory means that I have absolutely no idea what's going on, so I am just going to build a story and tell people, "*Here's what I think happened.*" A scientific theory is just a story built around science. *Not* a story that is *proven* by science. And here's the beauty of a theory . . . I don't have to prove it. I just have to make it up and rationalize it enough so that it sounds like it could work, and then it's up to you to prove it wrong. Isn't that beautiful? I can just make something up and I don't have to prove it right. You have to prove it wrong.

So here's the breakdown of the Darwinian theory of the evolution of man. You know the pictures. A monkey stands up more

and more until he goes from swinging in a tree eating bananas to wearing a business suit, driving a Beamer, and sipping lattes.

It's a great *theory*. In fact, many schools across America still teach this crap as truth. I know, how can I call this widely accepted theory "crap"? Easy. And it's not a feeling or a Christian freak-o belief. It's a facts thing. Let's get all scientific here.

1. Show me any other time when something changes species. See, the Darwinian theory claims that the monkey jumped species to make an entirely new and different one. I'll make it easy. We can start with some lower level creature. Humans and monkeys are pretty advanced. Show me any time where a cactus jumped over and became a pecan tree. Or show me how a fish jumped out of the water enough times that it became a bird. Go ahead, my little Darwinian Dum-Dums (a little reference to the suckers . . . uh . . . I mean, lollipops).

2. Show me the fossils! There are none. Oh, now, there are fossils before, after, and all around, but there are none that take us from monkey to man. Huge chunks of the evolutionary manuscript are missing. It's like someone erased that chapter from the book. Rather than argue that we haven't found that piece yet, just accept the fact that this piece doesn't exist.

Listen, I am not saying evolution is fake. It's as real as this book you are reading . . . or maybe this book is fake . . . anyway, evolution happens. But don't let the fact that someone said we came from monkeys and then others started to believe it change who you are. You were created. Your grandfather was created. And his g-pa and his and his all the way back to the first man. That's why there are no fossils. It's almost like man came out of nowhere . . . exactly! We were *not* here . . . we were *not* here . . . *poof!* We were here.

You are not an accident. You are here for a reason and with a purpose. You are going to hear a lot of theories, guesses, and people shouting, "Oh, I know what happened!" Go back to the Scripture. It says, "Test everything. Hold on to the good." That means the stuff you hear on TV, the stuff your teachers tell you, and the thoughts from your own little brain—don't just accept it because they call themselves experts. Test what they say. You will probably shoot holes all in their super-strong theories.

1 Thessalonians 5:21

National Geographic News Headline: "Chimps, Humans 96 Percent the Same, Gene Study Finds"

This means we come from monkeys, right? Well, not really, because "despite the similarities in human and chimp genomes, the scientists identified some 40 million differences among the three billion DNA molecules, or nucleotides, in each genome." That means the 4 percent difference is sooooo huge that this study still doesn't mean anything.

National Geographic News, August 31, 2005, Stefan Lovgren for National Geographic News, http://news.nationalgeographic.com/news/ 2005/08/0831_050831_chimp_genes.html

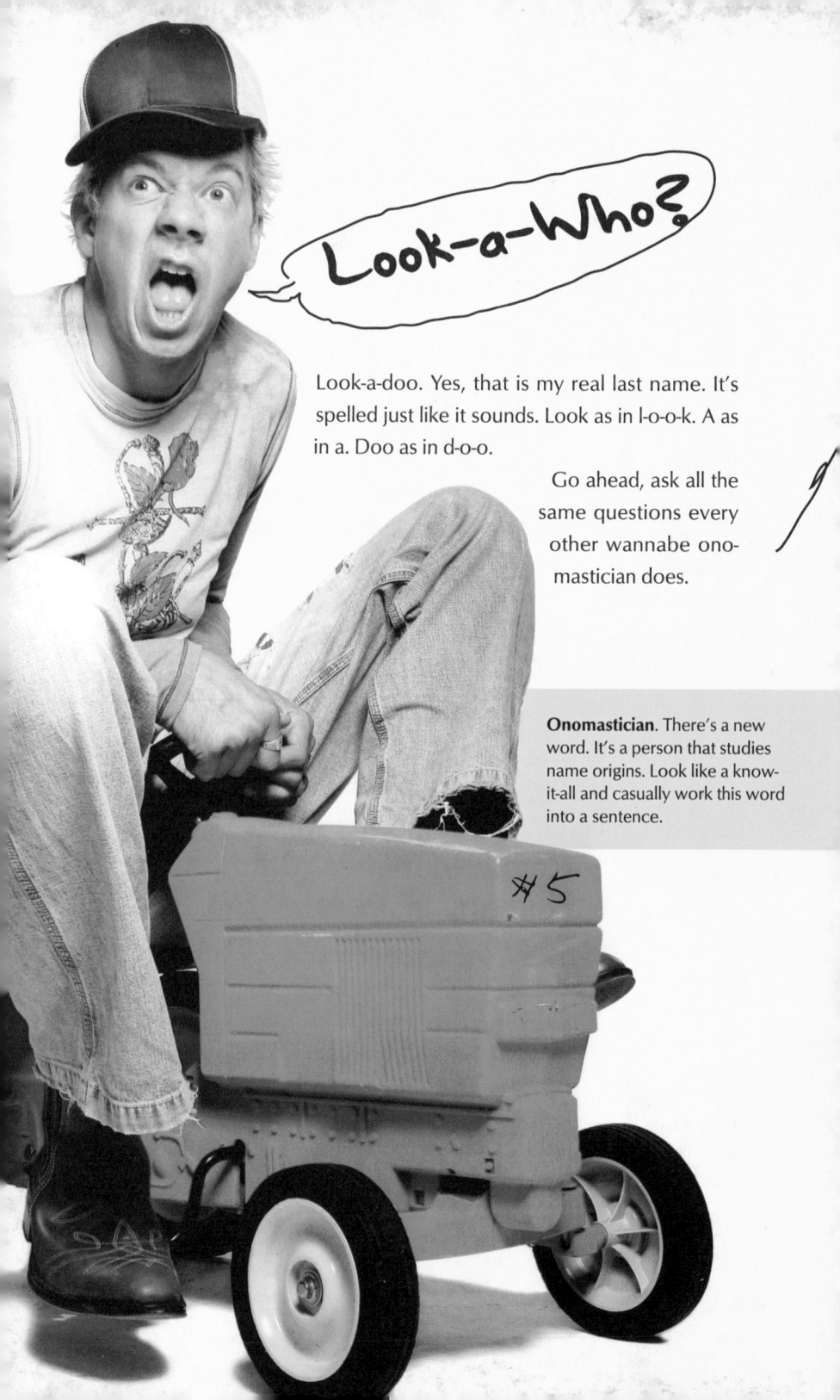

Look-a-Who?

Look-a-doo. Yes, that is my real last name. It's spelled just like it sounds. Look as in l-o-o-k. A as in a. Doo as in d-o-o.

Go ahead, ask all the same questions every other wannabe onomastician does.

Onomastician. There's a new word. It's a person that studies name origins. Look like a know-it-all and casually work this word into a sentence.

#5

Is ThaT really your lasT name?
Yes. Didn't we already cover that?

WhaT kind of name is Lookadoo?
It's a last name, duh.

Where did your name come from?
My dad.

Great. I'm glad I could clear up your questions for you.

Lookadoo is a great name. I love it . . . now. Growing up wasn't the best experience because of it. Well, I guess it wasn't that bad. Hey, when your real name is Lookadoo, any joke attempt sounds pretty lame. The real deal is funnier. I mean, c'mon, if someone wanted to cut me down, what name could they call me that was worse than what the teachers called me every day?

Names are cool. They are important. They tell who you are and who you belong to. And a name is something you have to live up to.

A name can be more than just the scribbles on your birth certificate or what your crazy aunt calls you at Christmas. It's a label. Something that someone else stuck on you. It could be something your family calls you. Shorty. Red. Stupid. Runt. It could be what a teacher called you. Lazy. Slacker. Something that someone said while making fun of you in gym class. Something someone said about you that stuck in your head. If it's still with you, it's because on some level you accepted it as part of your identity, your name.

What's cool is that God is all about changing names. Like when this dude named Saul was totally running around torturing and killing Christians, and God decided to have a little meeting with him. They had a talk,

"A good name is more desirable Than greaT riches" (Proverbs 22:1).

and Saul became the biggest, loudest preacher of Jesus as the Christ. Check it out in Acts 9. It's a pretty wicked story. Then he went around to the same places preaching for what he said he was totally against. And then in Acts 13, verse 9, it says, "Then Saul, who was also called Paul, filled with the Holy Spirit . . ." and that was it. He was called Paul from then on.

Same kinda deal with an OT guy named Abram. He was sold-out committed to God. And God wanted Abram to know that he was going to do some incredible things with him. So in Genesis 17:5–6, God said, "No longer will you be called Abram; your name will be Abraham, for I have made you a father of many nations. I will make you very fruitful," and it was done. His name was changed. His identity was changed and his destiny was changed.

And you know what? God doesn't just stop with changing the identity of ancient Bible people. He wants to change yours and give you a new one too. Your real identity. I'm telling you, if you get a new name, it will give you a new identity and will create a new destiny for you.

Right now, think back to your label that we were talking about before, an identity you've been given. Something that you believe about yourself or that someone else called you and it stuck with you. Jot it down.

OLD NAMES

It will probably be tough to look at, but remember, that's not you. It's what someone else stuck on you. Now, look at what you wrote, then shut your eyes. Clear out all distractions. Hibernate the lappie. Click off the tunes and then say something like this to God: *I know that's not how you see me. God, I want you to change my identity. How do you see me? Who am I to you? What do you call me?*

Then sit there in silence. I don't know how long. As long as it takes. Just sit there and see what starts popping into your head. And when something does, write it down. When you have some different names, some different labels, ask God, *Is this who I am to you?* And see what he says.

Then comes the good stuff. Once you get your new name, your new identity, you've got your ammo. The Enemy is going to try to hit you with your old, lame labels pretty quick. When that happens, you jump back with your new ID. And tell your own jacked-up mind that there's a new game in town. You are not that old name that someone put on you. Remind yourself of the name God gave you.

This will change who you are, and it will totally change where you go in life. Let go of the gunk and let God give you your name.

New names/labels

relational geometry 101

Ever been in a wobbly relationship? It seems so right in some ways and so wrong in others. To understand the dynamics that make a precarious pairing, you must go back to the foundational geometrics of relationships.

Relational Components

A relationship is made up of two individuals. Each individual is made up of three parts, as described in 1 Thessalonians 5:23. These are spirit, soul, and body.

spirit: taken from the Greek word *psych*, which in this case is referring to your mind, your intellect, your brain. This is the part that causes you to talk for hours and hours with your crush. It allows you to think about the other person. It is the part that gains knowledge that can help guide your dating life.

soul: from the Greek word *pneuma*, which means breath. For the Bible-day writers, your breath, your soul, was that thing that gave you a connection to the Creator. There are two types of souls:

living soul: those with a relationship with Christ

dead soul: those without a relationship with Christ

body: from the old school word *bod-a-bing*. Oh, never mind. I didn't look up body; you know what that is. Your physical, flesh-covered bod. The part you can touch, feel, smell, kiss.

Relational Construction

If you would have opened that geometry book that you kept hidden under your bed all semester, you would know that the strongest geometric shape is a triangle. Makes sense that the ancient pyramids are still standing. If you haven't taken geometry yet, then remember this. On the first day of school tell your teacher you don't need this class, and then blow her away with your knowledge. Then sit down and shut up. The class will be laughing at you.

Anyway, the strongest shape thing is true. And we, as humans, are made up of a triangular existence. Intellectual. Spiritual. Physical.

Now, if all three of these are at equal lengths and strengths, you are a complete and strong person. But let's say you are strong in the physical body area and in the spiritual body side, but intellectually you are absent. You have no brain. Then the triangle will be off balance and weak. The same with any of the legs. If you have the physical and the intellectual legs in place but you have no connection to the Creator through his Son Jesus, then you are a two-sided being that can be toppled and crushed. It is important to remember that we were created with a three-part design in place. The absence of any of them can destroy the entire person.

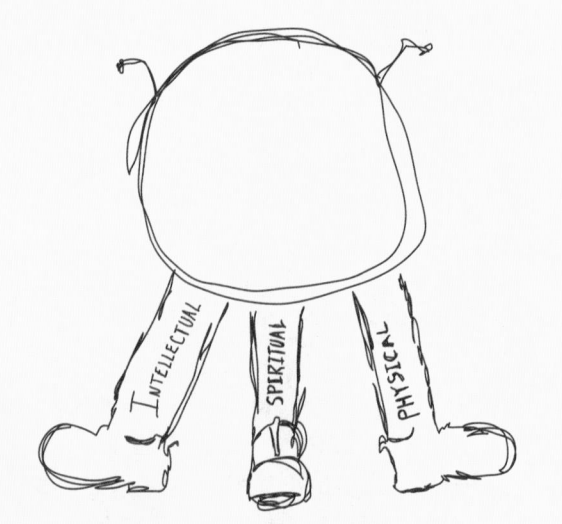

Relational Connection

Like connects to like. You have to have two individuals with all three components to have a strong relationship. The common misconception is that you can walk in with a super strong spiritual leg and compensate for someone with no spiritual leg—i.e., dating a nonbeliever. Well, it doesn't work that way. Like only connects to like. If two areas are not the same, then there is a major disconnect.

Examples:

s = spiritual
i = intellectual
p = physical

[spiritual—Intellectual and no body] + [s/i/b] = p/i/no p

The person you are trying to connect with *has no body*! You cannot get a great connection with a person who is not wrapped up in a body. So you cannot have a strong relationship.

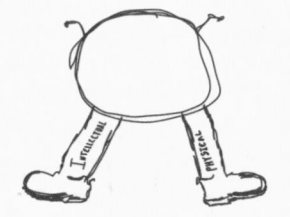

(p/i/s) + (p/I/no spiritual) = p/i

This person *has no spiritual leg*! This is as crazy as trying to hook up with someone who has no body. It just doesn't work.

Don't fool yourself into thinking that you will ever have a deep connection and stable relationship with someone who is not a believer. You only have two thirds of a relationship. Two legs of a triangle.

God made us to be strong. He made our relationships to be strong. So if you want to make sure that you are in the best position you can be in to find the perfect person, then don't date anyone without a body. Don't date anyone without a brain. And don't date anyone without a spirit. It sounds easy, but it's amazing how so many people start a relationship that is foundationally unsafe and then are shocked when it comes crumbling down.

> Do not be yoked together with unbelievers. For what do righteousness and wickedness have in common? Or what fellowship can light have with darkness?
>
> 2 Corinthians 6:14

If you are 60 or older, you understand what this Scripture means. For those who don't, I'll give you a mental picture to spy. A yoke wasn't the egg thing. It was a farm thing. It was the wood brace that connected two working animals together, like cows or oxen or something like that. Well, if you connect two animals together that are unequal, it won't work. Like if one is a super slow walker or even refuses to walk and the other is a fast walker, you are not going to get very far. That's what happens spiritually. If you are a follower of Christ and you connect to someone who is not a believer, then you are connected to someone walking in the opposite direction. You will be stuck.

Only connect with a solid three-part person. Then you will be able to have a solid relational foundation that will help you battle the bad times and totally enjoy the good ones.

#3 *Beauty Quest*

Girls, answer this question so that all of us stupid guys can understand a little more about how your brains work: Why do you go out and dump a big wad of cash for some shoes that you have to squeeze into? They hurt your feet from the moment you put them on, and then you tell yourself the same lie that they will be comfortable once you break them in. You know they won't. They look good and that's it. You will never have them on your feet long enough to break them in. In fact, most of the time you will carry another pair of shoes with you "just in case." Beauty at any cost . . . why, why, why?

In the same way, on the outside you appear
to people as righteous but on the inside
you are full of hypocrisy
and wickedness.

Matthew 23:28

Anyone give me an answer on this one. Why do we spend so much time trying to look good on the outside? New clothes, working out, fake-n-bake tan, hair, everything. We do everything we can to appear like we've got it all together when on the inside it's yuck-a-palooza. We are totally messed up with lying, sex, porn, drugs, anger, slashing people with our words, being rude—we are full of trash that just stinks up our life.

Listen, it's the inside that counts. Not the outside. Now, that doesn't mean stop bathing and brushing those dentals. It means spend some time on the inside. Work on stuff like trust, attitude, commitment, faith, love, kindness, compassion. Take a look at how long you spend each day getting together physically. Jot down the time. Then get a number for the amount of time you spend with God dealing with your inside. Compare the two. Let me guess, your mirror time is way bigger than your Jesus time, eh?

Don't rip yourself apart too much. It sucked when I did the numbers too. But you don't have to stay that way. You control your schedule and what you do when. Get to the important stuff. Shift a little more time toward working on the internal stuff that really matters. When you do that you will get hotter on the outside. Try it. It will work.

#2 Arachnophobia

I sat down in the principal's office after speaking at the school, and we were just chatting about the program, kids, and the state of America's youth when I noticed that sitting right next to me was the biggest, hairiest, ugliest spider I had ever seen in my life. It was in a glass cage, so I fought back the urge to scream like a little schoolgirl. As we sat there I stared at it and it stared at me.

I finally asked the principal about the angry-looking arachnid. She said it wasn't mean, it just looked that way. In fact, it was her pet. Her pet! C'mon, man, get a dog, a gerbil, maybe even a little bird, but a *spider*?

I asked her, "Do you play with it?" She said she could but she doesn't. And not because the spider would hurt her but because she could hurt the spider. She told me that the spider's legs are extremely delicate, and if she let anyone play with the spider, it could very easily get its leg broken. And if that happened, the spider could bleed to death. Not a bad option in my book, but hey, she's a spider fan.

You know, that's what the Word says about us and our actions and freedoms. Yeah, as a Christian we *can* do a lot of things. That doesn't mean we *should*. See, 1 Corinthians 10:23–24 spells it out pretty clear. "'Everything is permissible'—but not everything is beneficial. 'Everything is permissible'—but not everything is constructive. Nobody should seek his own good, but the good of others." Just because something isn't wrong, that doesn't make it right. If there is something that you think is totally okay but doing it could hurt someone else or cause them to stumble, then don't do it.

"Make up your mind not to put any stumbling block or obstacle in your brother's way."

Romans 14:13

#1 Ahhhh, our little Will. We first met Will at a music festival in Virginia. He was a tagalong and chauffeur for a friend. When we first met him we thought he was a little odd, but something about him was charming or attractive or something. We just couldn't figure it out.

We saw Will for the second time at another music festival I was speaking at. We needed help selling books and making sure I was where I was supposed to be at the right time, and Will was . . . he was still Will. Odd. Quirky. Different. And probably the coolest guy I have ever met.

Okay, Will had his moments. As soon as he got there, he got our truck stuck in the mud *and* got us lost. But I have to tell you, he was the perfect guy to have around. Will was not afraid to do anything. We needed tables moved, Will did it. Ran out of food, Will got it. Didn't have signs, Will made them. Needed to move the entire booth to another building, Will did it. Will was on top of things. I could walk away, go hop on stage and do my thing, and I didn't have to worry about anything. I knew Will had it under control.

The next time I saw Will was at our first Dateable Tour date. He picked me up at the airport wearing a vintage three-piece polyester suit complete with super-wide tie and shiny pleather shoes. He was a sight to behold. He was confident and secure and he was a blast.

He thought—well, we all thought—that this gig was going to run as smoothly as the other. Oh, but no. In just a few hours our venue cancelled out on us. The band broke their contract and didn't come, and our producer was a no-show. We were stuck. We had nothing . . . or so I thought. This was when Will became more than just odd, cool Will.

In the middle of this downward spiral, Will said, "*Hey, let's see what we do have. We have the speaker. We found a new venue. We have three movies, an iPod, and a bunch of CDs. Let's rewrite the program.*" Sounded crazy, but we were out of options. So we got busy. We had DVD players going. We were listening to music. We were adding stuff and taking stuff out of the program. We stayed up all night revamping the entire program.

When we got to the venue the next day, I told the sound guys to let Will run the show. They moved over and let him plug in all his gadgets and gizmos, and the show went on. And it was perfect. In fact, we had people come up to us and tell us that they were so glad the band didn't show up because it would have watered down the message. The same message that Will helped create the night before.

The next day Will drove two hours out of his way to get us to the airport. Will is the man. He will do whatever it takes to get the job done and to have an impact on people. Oh, and one other thing: Will is only 17 years old.

On our way home we were talking about how cool it would be if the world had more Wills. More young people who were excited, passionate, and connected with God and who had the confidence and attitude that they would do whatever it took to get the job done. And we started thinking about what we could do to

This is Will. ⟶
Honest.

help make that happen. That is when we came up with the Will-Doo Ministry.

Will-Doo is a true leadership training organization where we teach students to be like Will. We give them the skills and confidence to put together a Dateable Tour and let them be involved in something that is pure ministry where they can see the results. This is an incredible opportunity for you to be a part of something big.

As you read these words, you are close to finishing this book. Once you're done, you have some decisions to make. Are you going to continue to sit there and let life pass you by? Or are you going to take these random thoughts to heart? Are you going to live life with no regrets? Are you ready for that?

If you're done sitting down, if you're tired of standing still, it's time to step up and get moving. Be a part of something big. It can be going on a mission trip, coaching little kids' basketball, grabbing a bunch of buds and going through *The Hardest 30 Days of Your Life*, or connecting with the Will-Doo team. Whatever it is, put this book down, get out there, and make your own chapter. The next one is up to you. You get to write your own random thoughts about life, love, and relationships, but you have to get out there and live it. And when the world tries to keep you down, then go back to day one and remember 97 . . . and power through.

Will-Doo

If you are interested in being part of the team, we first need to give you a little warning. We're not looking for those of you who *think* you can do this or that it just sounds cool. This isn't for you. But if you want to hyper-charge your life and connect what you believe with what you live, then this may be your deal. We don't want those who are just okay with it. We want those of you that WILL-DOO it.

Apply to be a Will-Doo and start writing the next chapter of your book.

To apply for the Will-Doo Team, visit us at www.lookadoo.com and click on the Ministry Team link.

As you can see

by the evidence in your hands, Justin writes some really cool books. But his first love is being face-to-face speaking to groups. He has done everything from small group interactions to huge music festivals to throwing down at an event at the House of Blues. He has done nearly 3,500 programs to about half a million people. He would love to come speak at your event. And his wife is always willing to send him out of the house. He is perfect for school programs, conferences, retreats, parenting conferences, staff development, and all kinds of leadership and special events. Check out what Justin can do for you at www .lookadoo.com or email him and Emily directly at speakers@ lookadoo.com. But definitely check out the website.

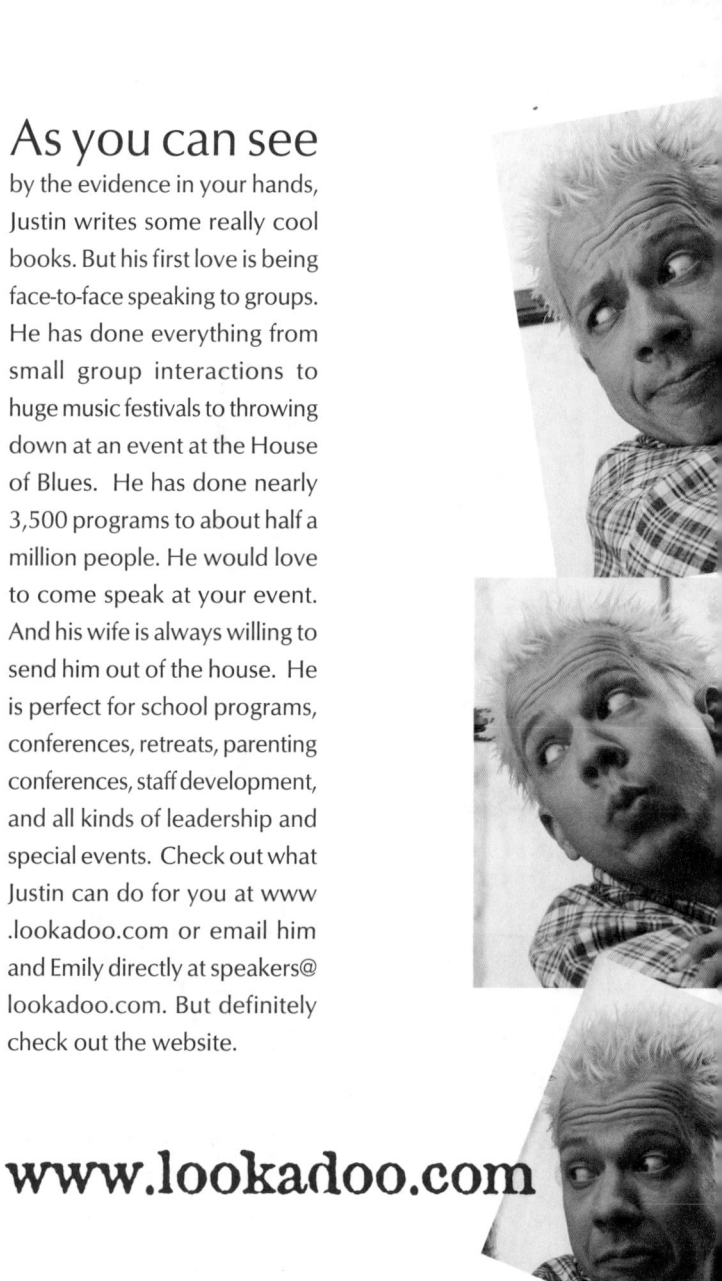

www.lookadoo.com